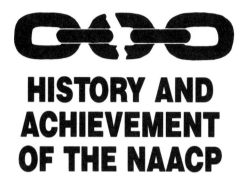

HISTORY AND ACHIEVEMENT OF THE NAACP

HISTORY

AND

ACHIEVEMENT

OF THE

NAACP

JACQUELINE L. HARRIS

The African-American Experience
Franklin Watts
New York   Chicago   London   Toronto   Sydney

Photographs copyright ©: The Bettmann Archive: pp. 1, 2 bottom, 5 top, 11 top; Cultural Resources, Raleigh, NC: p. 2 top; Illinois State Historical Library: p. 3; The Newberry Library, Chicago, IL: p. 4 top; Archives at the University of Massachusetts at Amherst: pp. 4 center & bottom, 5 center, 7 center; Library of Congress: pp. 5 bottom, 7 bottom; New York Public Library, Schomburg Center for Research in Black Culture: pp. 6 top, 10 top, 11 bottom, 13, 14 bottom; National Association for the Advancement of Colored People: pp. 6 bottom, 15 bottom, 16; The Kentucky Library, Western Kentucky University: p. 7 top ; UPI/Bettmann Newsphotos: pp. 8, 14 top, 15 top; Edna A. (Nixon) McIver: p. 9; AP/Wide World Photos: p. 10 bottom; Arkansas History Commission: p. 12 top; Department of the Army, U.S. Military Academy Archives: p. 12 bottom; M. Rudolph Vetter: p. 15 center.

Library of Congress Cataloging-in-Publication Data

Harris, Jacqueline L.
History and Achievement of the NAACP / Jacqueline L. Harris.
    p.   cm. — (African-American experience)
Includes bibliographical references and index.
Summary: Surveys the history of the National Association for the Advancement of Colored People and its achievements in the civil rights movement.
ISBN 0-531-11035-4
1. National Association for the Advancement of Colored People—History—Juvenile literature. 2. Afro-American—History—1877-1964—Juvenile literature. 3. Afro-Americans—Civil rights—Juvenile literature. 4. Civil rights movements—United States—History—20th century—Juvenile literature. [1. National Association for the Advancement of Colored People—History. 2. Afro-Americans—Civil rights. 3. Civil rights movements—History. 4. Race relations.] I. Title. II. Series.
                 E185.61.H26   1992
973′.0496073—dc20   92-8930 CIP AC

CONTENTS

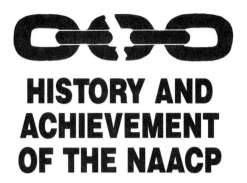

HISTORY AND
ACHIEVEMENT
OF THE NAACP

I

THE TIME BEFORE THE NAACP

It was the Fourth of July, 1852. Frederick Douglass, ex-slave, writer, scholar, and abolitionist, had been asked to give a speech in Rochester, New York. In that speech, he said: "What to the American slave is your Fourth of July? I answer; a day that reveals to him more than all other days in the year, the gross injustice and cruelty to which he is the constant victim. . . . [T]he existence of slavery in this country brands your republicanism as a sham, your humanity as base pretense, and your Christianity as a lie. It destroys your moral power abroad; it corrupts your politicians at home. . . . It is the antagonistic force in your government, the only thing that seriously disturbs and endangers your Union."[1]

Douglass's words were prophetic. On April 12, 1861, Confederate batteries opened fire on Fort Sumter in the Charleston, South Carolina, harbor. North and South, bitterly divided over the issue of slavery, went to war. The Civil War had begun.

By the summer of 1862, it had become apparent

that the conflict that many had thought would be settled in ninety days could well go on for years. Originally, the North's goal had been to save the Union—to conquer the Confederate states and bring them back into the fold. But most northerners believed that slavery was the root cause of the war. If the war was to go on, victory must result in the end of slavery.

On New Year's Day, 1863, President Abraham Lincoln issued the Emancipation Proclamation, which declared that all slaves in the Confederate rebel states were free. The Proclamation did not immediately free any slaves, however. Only when the Union troops occupied the South could it be enforced. But now the war had become a war for freedom. When the Union victory ended the war in 1865, Congress passed the Thirteenth Amendment to the Constitution, freeing all slaves and abolishing slavery.

The postwar period of Reconstruction began. Four million slaves found themselves free and also facing the kinds of responsibilities freedom imposed—finding food, shelter, and jobs in the devastated South. They needed so much to make all of this possible. They needed education, denied to slaves by law in many states. They needed protection from an embittered South. They needed land to farm.

The Freedman's Bureau, established in March 1865 by the government just before the war ended, was there to assist blacks and whites made destitute by the war and slavery. The Bureau provided food and medical care and set up schools. The Bureau staff ensured that job or purchase contracts between ex-slaves and former slave owners were set up fairly.

Within four years, Bureau staff members had issued 21 million meal rations (a week's supply of food), set up forty hospitals, and spent $2 million treating 450,000 patients. They found homes for thirty thousand families and helped many ex-slaves obtain farms through the Homestead Act of 1866. They reunited families separated by the war or slavery. Many slave families had been split apart when some members were sold.

The Bureau established four thousand schools, among them a number of black universities—including Howard University in Washington, D.C., Talladega (Alabama) University, Atlanta (Georgia) University, and Fisk University in Nashville, Tennessee. Ten thousand teachers were recruited to teach the 250,000 black students who flocked to the schools. Everything, from reading, writing, and mathematics to sewing, carpentry, and agriculture, was taught.

In 1866, Congress passed the Civil Rights Act, which forbade discrimination on account of race, targeting southern state laws called Black Codes, a carryover from slave days. Black Codes were aimed at keeping ex-slaves "down" by limiting their rights. The codes said that black people could not testify against white people in court, could not marry white people, and could not travel freely. One code said that any person without a job was a vagrant and could be arrested. If the person could not pay a $50 fine, he or she was hired out to an employer, who paid the fine. Blacks could actually be fined for using insulting gestures or for preaching without a license. The Act outlawing these Black Codes was to be enforced by the Freedman's Bureau and the occupying federal troops.

In 1868, Congress passed the Fourteenth Amendment, which made former slaves citizens. In 1870, the Fifteenth Amendment gave the new male citizens the right to vote. Suddenly, the whole promise of American citizenship unfolded before the ex-slaves: voting, moving about freely, and taking part in the government were now theirs.

Between 1870 and 1871, Congress passed several enforcement acts to guarantee the vote and the rights of black people. Throughout the South, black voters protected by federal troops went to the polls and voted ex-Confederates out of office. Blacks—and whites who supported the rights of blacks—were voted into state offices. Black citizens helped draft state constitutions and put in place the first comprehensive education systems in the South. Black men served as lieutenant governor in South Carolina, Mississippi, and Louisiana. Two blacks represented the state of Mississippi in the U.S. Senate, and twenty blacks represented South Carolina, Mississippi, and Florida in the House of Representatives.

The Act of February 28, 1871, was intended to protect blacks from terrorist groups when the state was unwilling or unable to do so. Groups such as the Ku Klux Klan, the Knights of the White Camellia, the White Line, and the White Brotherhood were born out of white resentment of blacks. Said one white planter of blacks, "We can't feel toward them as you do—they've always been our owned servants and we've been used to having them mind us."

The Ku Klux Klan, wearing white robes and hoods, rode out at night terrorizing blacks. Their goal was "to keep our Negroes under control." William Coleman, an ex-slave who had become a successful farmer in Mississippi, described a visit from the Ku Klux Klan in testimony to a Congressional committee:

Well I don't know anything that I said or done that had injured anyone.... [T]hey came about a half an hour before day.... [T]hey were shooting and going on at me through the house.... [N]one of the shots hit me but they aimed to hit me.... [T]hey told me they rode from Shiloh in two hours and came to kill me.... [T]hey took me out to the big road before my gate, whipped me until I couldn't move or holler or do nothing, but just lay there like a log.... [T]hey left me there for dead.... [T]hey told me "When you meet a white man in the road, lift your hat. I'll learn you that you are a nigger and not to be going around like you thought yourself a white man."

Coleman told of three black friends also visited by the Klan. Why were they whipped? Coleman answered, "I don't know. They said it was because they had land. They had got too big. They say when you get land or a mule or a horse, they want to kill you for getting above your business. Or they want to drive you away."[2]

Groups such as the Klan became a kind of underground movement, approved of and condoned by those Southerners who wanted to maintain black people in a slavelike situation. The only hope for freed slaves was the federal government and the protection it could provide. Congress had already passed the laws to protect them; those laws had to be enforced. In 1875, a law was passed that would lead to events that would have a profound effect on the federal support blacks needed.

The Civil Rights Act of 1875 made it a crime to deny service to blacks or to segregate them from other patrons in hotels, restaurants, theaters, and trains. The act read, in part, "All persons within the jurisdiction of the United States shall be entitled to the full and equal enjoyment of the accommodations of inns, public conveyances on land or water, theatre and other places of public amusement." The act called for a fine or imprisonment for violators.

In Louisville, Kentucky, in Washington, D.C., and in Chicago, black people were admitted to theaters and hotels previously barred to them. But despite the new law, many people were refused service in other cities. Many people sued to claim their rights. The suits piled up in federal district courts. Finally, one case was submitted to the U.S. Supreme Court.

On October 15, 1883, the high court handed down a ruling that sounded the death knell for the Congressional protection and guarantee of civil rights for black people. The court found two sections of the 1875 Civil Rights Act unconstitutional, ruling that neither the Thirteenth nor the Fourteenth Amendment called for federal regulation of social discrimination. In announcing the ruling, Justice Joseph P. Bradley said that the Thirteenth, Fourteenth, and Fifteenth amendments, passed to aid the freed slave, must have some limits. The black, he said, must cease to be "the special favorite of the law" and "assume the rank of a mere citizen." Only one justice, Justice John Harlan, dissented. He argued that a section in the Thirteenth Amendment guaranteed "universal civil freedom" and that discrimination violated that civil freedom. The Fourteenth Amendment, he said, gave Congress the power to ban state action that denied liberty or equality. He noted that railroads, innkeepers, and managers of other public accommodations were considered agents of the state.[3]

In 1896, the Court followed up this ruling in *Plessy* v. *Ferguson,* upholding railroad segregation laws passed by eight southern states. In 1906, the Court upheld laws calling for segregated education in public schools. Again and again Congress was seeing its efforts to protect the rights of blacks undercut by the Supreme Court. The Civil Rights Act of 1875 would be the last piece of civil rights legislation passed by Congress until 1957.

Other events contributed to the death knell for the civil rights of black people. Terrorist groups such as the Ku Klux Klan frightened blacks away from the polls. Black officeholders were voted out. In some cases, whites didn't bother with the ballot. They used the bullet to rid themselves of blacks holding state elected office.

In a deal for electoral votes struck during the presidential election of 1876, Rutherford B. Hayes assumed office in exchange for ordering the withdrawal of federal troops from the South. The Freedman's Bureau, charged with enforcing the Civil Rights Acts but lacking the support of President Andrew Jackson, had been abolished in 1872. Thus in 1877, as federal troops boarded the trains for the North, they took with them the last means of enforcing the amendments and laws passed to guarantee the rights of blacks. The federal government had in effect abandoned black people to the southern states.

States began to pass one "Jim Crow," or segregation, law after another. While such laws predominated in the South, many northern states also passed segregation laws. Whites and blacks were forbidden to shake hands or share a table in a restaurant. Blacks were denied rooms in hotels. They had to enter public buildings, banks, and theaters through a rear, "colored" entrance. Blacks sat in the back of the bus, while whites sat in the front. Special rail coaches for blacks were placed behind the noisy, smoky train locomotive. There were separate "colored" and "white" restrooms, waiting rooms, even drinking fountains. Churches, schools, cemeteries, barber shops, and mortuaries were segregated. The only jobs open to most blacks were menial ones such as porter, maid, cook, laundress, or chauffeur. Housing was segregated.

Grandfather clauses inserted into the voting laws of Mississippi, Louisiana, Oklahoma, and other states were aimed at the disfranchisement of black people. These clauses said that anyone whose ancestors had voted before the enactment of the Fifteenth Amendment was excused from taking a stringent literacy test and qualified to vote. Since most blacks had been slaves or descended from slaves, and teaching a slave to read was illegal, this rule robbed them of their right to vote. Gerrymandering (redividing election districts), violence, poll taxes (charging a tax to voters), and secretly moving polling places also were used to keep blacks from voting.

The lynch mobs began their bloody work. Seizing a black person jailed for a crime, the mob would drag that person out of jail and deliver its own brand of justice—stabbing, shooting, and sometimes burning the person alive. Sometimes the target of the mob was a black person who was simply in the wrong place at the wrong time.

In Memphis in 1892, a mob took three black grocery store owners from a jail where they had been unjustly held and shot them to death. The last words of one of the murdered men were, "Tell my people to go West—there is no justice for them here."[4] Hundreds of black Memphis residents sold their property and did just that. At the urging of their ministers, two entire church congregations packed up and left. Memphis soon began to miss the many black workers and consumers who left.

As the years passed, other blacks would flee the repression of the South, heading west or north. But they would find discrimination, segregation, and lynch mobs there too.

II

THE FOUNDING OF
THE NAACP

Springfield, the Illinois state capital, was in 1908 the business center for the surrounding farm communities and had a reputation for being one of the most corrupt cities in the Midwest. Reported the Chicago *Daily News,* "Vice and other forms of law-breaking have been given a wide latitude. The notoriety of Springfield's evil resorts has been wide-spread."[1] Springfield was also the birthplace of Abraham Lincoln, the Great Emancipator.

It was to cities in Illinois such as Springfield, Peoria, and Chicago, as well as to many other northern cities, that many blacks migrated from the oppressive South. They came looking for the homes and jobs denied them in the South. Many whites resented blacks because they felt that they had come to take their jobs. Some blacks barred from joining unions signed up as strikebreakers, filling in on jobs abandoned by workers on strike. This further embittered white workers.

On August 14, 1908, citizens of Springfield glancing at their morning papers discovered that within the space of five weeks two black men had been accused of and jailed for rape. By early afternoon, groups of angry whites started to gather around outside the jail. By 5 P.M., four thousand people were milling around outside the jail. The sheriff, who was concerned for his prisoners, had the two men moved out of the rear entrance and transported by car and train to the safety of the state prison in Bloomington.

By sundown, the crowd had become an angry mob. When the mob discovered that the black prisoners weren't in the jail, it set out to punish Harry Loper, a white man and the person who was rumored to have driven the prisoners to the train. Loper owned a restaurant five blocks away. The mob marched on the restaurant. Several men overturned Loper's car. Someone threw a brick through the restaurant's plate glass window. Shouting such threats as "Curse the day that Lincoln freed the nigger," "Niggers must depart from Springfield," and "Abe Lincoln brought them to Springfield, we drive them out," the mob then looted, destroyed, and burned Loper's restaurant. In the ensuing riot, one waiter was killed, and many bystanders and police officers were injured.

Now blacks became the mob's target. The angry mob beat black porters at the railroad station, dragged blacks from streetcars and beat them, and wrecked and torched nearly every building and home in the nearby black residential district. By 1 A.M., most of the eastern end of the city was in flames. When whites began to torch his home, one black elderly man fired into the crowd in defense of himself and his home. Whites shot him, dragged his body through the streets, and hung him from a lamppost. An eighty-four-year-old black shoemaker who was married to a white woman was dragged from his yard, hung from a tree, and hacked to death with knives.

Only the arrival of the state militia put a stop to

the murder and arson. The toll was enormous and tragic. Two black people had been lynched. Four white people had been killed by stray bullets, and fifty black people were severely injured. Scores of homes and buildings in the black section of town had been destroyed.

By early morning, Springfield resembled a city devastated by war. Soldiers had pitched tents on the green. Horse soldiers patrolled the streets. A pall of smoke hung over the ruined east side of the city.

In the aftermath, under pressure from anonymous threats, many companies fired their black employees. Jobless and homeless, blacks left the city by the thousands, some by train, some on foot, heading north and west. Some Illinois towns such as Peoria and Jacksonville refused to allow the black refugees into their city limits. A black baby died of exposure as her parents walked west toward St. Louis. Ironically, one of the black men accused of rape was exonerated when his accuser came forth and admitted that she had been attacked by a white man.

Springfield was not ashamed. Most of the white citizens condoned the action of the mob. "Why the niggers came to think they were as good as we are," said one man. The *Illinois State Journal* wrote that "the riot was caused by black misconduct, inferiority and unfitness for free institutions."[2]

In a Sunday sermon, a minister suggested that denying the vote to blacks would solve the problem. State newspapers blamed Springfield's lax law enforcement, foreign immigrants, and blacks. Most southern papers gloated over the northern riot. However, the St. Louis *Post Dispatch* wrote: "It was one of the worst race riots that ever disgraced the country and the disgrace is the more humiliating in that the outrages were perpetrated under the very shadow of Lincoln's tomb."[3]

The tragic riot drew the attention of William English Walling, a wealthy Kentucky writer who had traveled with his wife to Springfield to see for himself why the riot had happened. Walling's wife was Jewish and had suffered at the hands of Russian anti-Semites. What they discovered convinced the Wallings that Springfield's hatred of blacks was far worse than Russian hatred of the Jews.[4]

In searching for the root causes of Springfield's hatred of blacks, Walling looked through past issues of the local newspapers. He found that in subtle and not-so-subtle ways, the local press had inflamed white racism. News reports and editorials had suggested links between crime and blacks and endorsed the South's treatment of blacks.[5]

Walling wrote an article for *The Independent,* a publication that had long been a defender of human rights, in which he expressed his shock at Springfield's shamelessness and its approval of the terrorist acts of the mob. He described the political and business boycott intended to drive all blacks out of the city. This amounted to a kind of reward to the mob. Abandoned black property, jobs, and businesses were the booty of their terrorism. Bigotry would run the city, become the guiding principle. Other cities might follow suit. Walling saw such a situation as a prelude to the death of the political democracy that underlay the country's system of government. He believed that a situation in which one group's unfounded hatred of another could literally force that group out of the mainstream of American society would mean the degeneration of that society.

"Who realizes the seriousness of the situation? What large and powerful body of citizens is ready to come to the Negro's aid?" he asked.[6]

Mary White Ovington responded to Walling by letter within an hour after she had read his article.

Ovington, a social worker and the wealthy grand-daughter of a white abolitionist, had more or less dedicated her life to "the Negro and his problem."

Walling, Ovington, and Henry Moskowitz, another white social worker, met at Walling's New York City apartment during the first week of January 1909. Walling described his idea of a national biracial organization of "fair-minded whites and intelligent blacks" that would address the wrongs endured by black people. The three decided that a statement of the injustices suffered by black people should be drafted, calling for a conference to be held later in the year. The statement would carry the signatures of prominent educators, social workers, and writers. It would be issued on Lincoln's birthday, February 12, 1909.

Three white people—a Jew, a Southerner, and the granddaughter of an abolitionist—had taken the first steps that would result in the organization known today as the National Association for the Advancement of Colored People—the NAACP.

Others were recruited to join the effort, including two black clergymen, Bishop Alexander Walters of the African Methodist Episcopal Zion Church and the Reverend William Henry Brooks of St. Mark's Methodist Episcopal Church of New York. Other prominent whites agreed to be a part of the organization. These included Lillian Wald and Florence Kelley, two social workers; William Russell, a writer and the Wallings' close friend; and Oswald Garrison Villard, grandson of abolitionist William Lloyd Garrison and publisher of the *New York Evening Post.*

Villard had grown up proud of his grandfather and his work to abolish slavery. He could wish for nothing more than to carry on the Garrison tradition of seeking justice for black people. Of his being asked to join, Villard said, "No greater compliment has ever been paid to me. . . . [W]ith such a body we could instantly handle any discrimination against the Negro and carry the case, if necessary to a higher court."[7]

Villard was asked to write what would be entitled *The Call,* intended to announce that an organization was to be formed and to recruit those interested in joining the effort. *The Call* proposed an organization that "should be an aggressive watchdog of Negro liberties that would allow no wrong to take place without a protest and pressure to right the wrong." It cited such injustices to black people as "disfranchising the Negro," "being set apart in trains in which they pay first class fares for third class service," the states' declining "to do their elementary duty in preparing the Negro through education for the best exercise of citizenship," "the spread of lawless attacks upon the Negro, often accompanied by revolting brutalities." *The Call* concluded: "Silence under these conditions means tacit approval. Hence we call upon all believers in democracy to join in a national conference for the discussion of present evils, the voicing of protests, and the renewal of the struggle for civil and political liberty."[8] Sixty prominent people signed it. It was sent to a number of newspapers, but few published it or even mentioned it. (See Appendix A for a complete text of *The Call.*)

One person not invited to sign *The Call* was Booker T. Washington. Washington, an ex-slave, had founded Tuskegee Institute with the support of the Freedman's Bureau. Washington was considered by many to be the leader of the ten million blacks in America. Presidents, governors, congressmen, scholars, and philanthropists consulted him when they wanted the support of blacks, wanted to help them, or needed a measure of black opinion.

Washington believed that blacks had to earn the right to be citizens. In an address to the Atlanta Exposition on September 18, 1895, Washington said:

The wisest among my race understand that the agitation of questions of social equality is the extremest folly, and that progress in enjoyment of all the privileges that will come to us must be the result of severe and constant struggle, rather than of artificial forcing. No race that has anything to contribute to the markets of the world is long in any degree ostracized. It is important and right that all privileges of the law be ours, but it is vastly more important that we be prepared for the exercise of those privileges. The opportunity to earn a dollar in a factory just now is worth infinitely more than the opportunity to spend a dollar in an opera house.[9]

The Call was seeking just what Washington opposed—an organized aggressive public campaign to win the civil and political rights of blacks.

The Negro National Conference, described in *The Call,* was set for May 31 and June 1, 1909, in New York City. One thousand invitations were mailed out. Villard wrote a special invitation to Washington. Villard, who had once been a supporter of Washington but had become critical of his policies, did not really want Washington to attend the conference. In his invitation to Washington, Villard described the new organization as aggressive, one that would fight for the rights of black people. Washington, he wrote, would be welcome at the meeting, but his failure to attend would be understood. Washington replied, "I fear my presence might restrict freedom of discussion and might also tend to make the conference go in directions which it would not like to go."[10]

Three hundred people attended the meeting. A keynote speech by William Hayes Ward, editor of *The Independent,* set the stage. "The purpose of this conference is to reemphasize in word, and so far as is possible in act, the principle that equal justice should be done to man as man and particularly to the Negro,"

Ward said. He pointed out that one key to the problem was that many white Southerners believed blacks to be physically and mentally inferior to whites, or less than human, and thought they could never be contributing members of American society.[11]

Several scientists then made presentations that refuted the idea that blacks were inferior. Livingstone-Farrand, a Columbia University anthropologist, and Burt G. Wilder, a Cornell University zoologist, demonstrated that there is no difference between the brains of blacks and whites. Edwin R. A. Seligman showed that the environment had prevented the advancement of blacks. "All that was needed to enable the black to contribute to society was opportunity, full, fair, and free," said philosopher John Dewey, also a participant in the conference.[12]

William E. B. DuBois, a black writer and Atlanta University professor, pinpointed the problems for blacks as political and economic. Blacks needed the vote, he said. Blacks needed education and the right to move freely about their country, enjoying the rights and privileges of other citizens. Blacks needed their civil rights. Without rights, blacks were objects of contempt, which destroyed their self-respect and forced them into "a new slavery."[13]

Other speakers described solutions to the problems DuBois and others had outlined. Encourage a favorable public opinion of blacks, work to get laws that ban lynching, work for the reduction of representation in Congress for southern states that denied the vote to blacks, get federal aid for education, and build an organization to do this work.

Villard described the organization he thought should be formed. Its mission would be that of watchdog for the rights of blacks. It would be an incorporated national organization that would exist on donations of money. It would be an organization of blacks and whites, working together to make the nation live up to its democratic ideal of equality. The organization would publicize black achievements and investigate and publicize lynchings and other injustices. Teams of lawyers would pursue the punishment of lynchers and work to ensure the enforcement of the Fourteenth and Fifteenth amendments, which gave blacks the vote and made them citizens. The lawyers would also fight to overturn laws that denied the vote and civil rights to blacks. The organization would have special departments to deal with education, labor, housing, and landowning.

On the last day of the meeting, the attendees appointed a Committee of Forty that would form the new organization. Villard wrote a number of resolutions for the approval of the attendees that demanded equal civil and educational rights; the right to work; and protection against violence, murder, and intimidation. The resolution also criticized President William Howard Taft for his lack of support for enforcement of the Fifteenth Amendment.

The attendees struggled until well past midnight settling on the language of the resolutions. Several black attendees took issue with practically every sentence. In this wrangling, some of the whites sensed suspicion and doubt among blacks. "I suppose we really ought not to blame these poor people, who have been tricked so often by white men, for being suspicious," Villard would later write in a report to his uncle William Lloyd Garrison, Jr.[14]

DuBois described that last night as one of burning earnestness as "the black mass moved forward . . . to take charge."[15] They wanted to make a public statement, they were uncertain of how one formed an organization, and suspicious of the whites' wish to help them. Finally, they put their trust in Villard, grandson of the great abolitionist, and voted for his plan.

And so as the meeting ended, the attendees had finally agreed that the new organization would pursue the struggle for civil and political liberty for blacks as set forth in *The Call.* But they had not yet named their new organization. Throughout the coming months, the small group of founders would consider such names as Committee on the Negro and Committee on the Status of the Negro. But finally the word "advancement," which Villard had used constantly when describing the organization's goals, provided the inspiration for the name the founders felt was appropriate. By May 1910, the name for the new organization had been chosen: the National Association for the Advancement of Colored People. Its goal was to achieve equal rights and opportunities for all black people. Its major activities were to provide legal aid, conduct mass meetings, investigate wrongs to blacks, and publicize wrongs and victories.

To give it the power to act as a body, the NAACP was incorporated in the state of New York in June 1911. The incorporators included Villard, DuBois, and Ovington. Wrote Ovington: "Our future I am sure will be one of great responsibility and great accomplishment. I think it will prove that we were right in our first conception of the organization that it should be a gathering together throughout the country of men and women, no matter what their race or color, who believed there should be no race distinctions in this country."[16]

They were revolutionaries, for in 1910, demands that blacks vote in Mississippi, that lynching, even in the South, be outlawed, and that segregation be abolished were revolutionary.

III

**GETTING ORGANIZED
AND BRANCHING OUT**

The new organization set up its first office in the *New York Evening Post* building, courtesy of Oswald Villard, the NAACP chairman and publisher of the *Post.* Morefield Storey, a nationally known white lawyer and friend of abolitionist Charles Sumner, was the president. Joining the executive committee at this point was wealthy white New Yorker Joel Spingarn, who had been chairman of Columbia's Department of Comparative Literature. Together the chairman, the president, and the executive committee set and administered policy. Mary Ovington was elected executive secretary, in charge of running the main office.

Now began the job of building the organization and fulfilling its mission of legal action and publicity. Anyone who wished to join in the work of demanding equal rights for black people could be a member. Dues were $500 for life members, $100 for donors, $2 for contributors, and $1 for associate members. Group memberships for clubs, lodges, and churches were also available. Other sources of funding besides membership fees would come from large donations from the wealthy and from the publication and sale of pamphlets.

At first, Storey, Joel Spingarn's brother, Arthur B. Spingarn, and Arthur Spingarn's law partner, Charles Studin, handled the legal work from their own law offices without charging a fee. Not until 1936 was the organization able to hire its own lawyer, Charles H. Houston, a brilliant black attorney.

In July 1910, William E. B. DuBois was asked to join as Director of Publications and Research. In 1905, he had founded the all-black Niagara Movement, an organization dedicated to opposing Booker T. Washington's views and working to fight segregation and discrimination. The organization had lasted only a few years, falling prey to internal disagreements. Many members of the Niagara Movement had later joined the NAACP. As one who had long subscribed to the principles on which the NAACP had been founded, DuBois would make many important contributions.

DuBois had worked in many interracial groups before. "Ordinarily," he said, "the white members of a committee become dominant. Either by superior training or their influence or their wealth they take charge . . . and use the colored membership as their helpers. . . . If the Negroes attempt to dominate and conduct the committee, the whites become dissatisfied and gradually withdraw. In the NAACP, it became our primary effort to achieve an equality of racial influence without stressing race and without allowing undue predominance to either group."[1]

Villard and other members were distressed by "the way colored people fight among themselves."[2] The fights seemed to be linked to a struggle for status among people for whom there were few opportunities for prestige. The average black person of the day, on the other hand, tended to be apathetic and uninterested in the struggle being undertaken by the NAACP.[3] Novelist Jesse Fauset wrote to Joel Spingarn, "Prod us, prick us, goad us on by unpleasant truths to ease off this terrible outer self of sloath and acceptance. . . . [S]ome of us need to be told that we should be men. . . . [D]on't give up on us . . . for we are worth it."[4]

DuBois began work on the NAACP magazine, which would be called *The Crisis*. The first issue, published in November 1910, pledged itself to "set forth those facts and arguments which show the danger of race prejudice, particularly as manifested today toward colored people."[5] It contained news, editorials, book reviews, and reports on NAACP activities. Among the departments in the magazine was a section called "The Burden" that described cases of racial injustice. Other articles focused on issues other than injustice against blacks—urging black women to become involved in the struggle for the women's right to vote. Wrote DuBois, "As often as I could afford, I portrayed the faces and features of colored folk. One cannot realize today how rare that was in 1910. The colored papers carried few or no illustrations; the white papers none (of black people). In many great periodicals, it was a standing rule that no Negro portrait was to appear."[6]

The first issue of *The Crisis* was seven by ten inches in size and sixteen pages long. DuBois printed one thousand copies. From the first, it was a phenomenal success. By the end of its first year, *The Crisis* had ten thousand subscribers. By the tenth year, circulation was one hundred thousand! Clearly, the world was hungry for news on the civil rights front.

In addition to editing *The Crisis*, DuBois looked for ways to stimulate black pride and self-esteem. He researched African history and black folklore and songs. He wrote up his research and presented it in speeches.

The NAACP also looked for other ways to build

black pride. In 1913, Joel Spingarn, the chairman of the board, endowed a gold medal—the Spingarn Medal. Each year the medal would be awarded to honor "the highest and noblest achievement of an American Negro." In February 1915, Ernest Just, a Howard University scientist, became the first Spingarn medalist. The Spingarn Medal became a major mark of achievement in the black world.

The NAACP persuaded New York state to sponsor the Negro Exposition. Held in 1913, the exposition celebrated the fiftieth anniversary of the Emancipation Proclamation and featured exhibits and presentations demonstrating the progress made by blacks since the Emancipation Proclamation was signed. DuBois wrote and directed a pageant called "The Star of Ethiopia." Nearly thirty thousand people attended.

In the early years of the twentieth century, there was no radio or television to carry firsthand immediate news of the NAACP and its work and to recruit people for the work. Lectures and mass meetings were used to get out the message. Special anniversaries such as Lincoln's birthday, the birthday of the famous abolitionist William Lloyd Garrison, or the anniversary of the signing of the Emancipation Proclamation were commemorated with mass meetings. DuBois estimated that during his first ten years with the NAACP he traveled in nearly every state and gave more than four hundred lectures to audiences totaling two hundred thousand people.

In 1913, working with May Nerney, who had succeeded Mary Ovington as NAACP executive secretary, a team of white volunteer journalists formed a press committee. They supplied newspapers and magazines with accurate, well-documented information on issues related to blacks. NAACP investigative reports on lynching or segregation were sent to the media. Within a few years the NAACP was providing information to a list of 289 newspapers—white, black, northern, southern, and foreign.

The publication of *The Crisis*, the lectures, and the mass meetings were intended to spread the word about the NAACP and its mission and to inspire people to become members. In March 1911, the total membership of the NAACP was 179, and most of the members belonged to the national office. Now began the branching out. The association began recruiting vigilance committees, which were supposed to be vigilant to cases of local racial injustice and to act to right the wrong. The local organizations eventually became branches with many of the same responsibilities—reducing racial prejudice and contributing to the advancement of blacks—as the national office. The branches looked to the national board for policy and sent part of their dues to the national office.

Branches were required to include white members. The national office was insistent on white membership for three reasons: to lend prestige and help raise money, to neutralize the opinions of white southerners, and to promote understanding between blacks and whites. Above all, the national office tried to make new branches understand the question of civil rights as it related to democracy: that discrimination and segregation had no place in a democratic society. However much it might degrade a black person to feel the sting of racial injustice, there was a bigger goal to strive for—to make the nation live up to its democratic ideal. Achieving this would mean cutting across all areas and instances of racial injustice, from lynching to being denied a job or a seat in a theater.

As the branches were organized and went to work, gradually the goals and work of the NAACP began to have a national impact. The first branch was organized in New York City as the New York Vigilance Committee. Among the members were NAACP attorney

Arthur Spingarn and NAACP co-founder Mary Ovington, also members of the national organization. Its mission was to investigate and initiate legal action in cases of racial violence or discrimination. Publicity encouraged black people to report injustices to the branch headquarters.

During its first six months, the New York committee dealt with and successfully secured justice in cases of police brutality and discrimination. A policeman was brought to trial and suspended from his job for three months. In cases in which blacks were refused admission to a theater and to an amusement park, successful legal action was brought against the managements.

The Boston branch was formed in 1912. The city was once the center of the effort to abolish slavery. Many of the descendants of abolitionists quite naturally became members of the NAACP, an organization some called the New Abolitionists. Notable black intellectuals such as attorney Butler Wilson and Clement G. Morgan also joined the branch.

The Bostonians went right to work, earning in 1913 the right for blacks to swim at the YMCA. They held a mass meeting at Fanueil Hall to protest segregation in the federal government. Meetings such as these alerted black people to injustices against black people and the means of fighting injustice. Branch members succeeded in getting a songbook containing the words "darky," "nigger," and "massa" withdrawn from the Boston school system.

In 1915, the Boston branch worked to prevent the showing of the movie *Birth of a Nation.* The film portrayed black men as dangerous brutes whose single wish was to possess white women. Members felt that this false portrayal would build up dangerous antagonisms between whites and blacks. The branch brought its case to the mayor of Boston. The mayor, citing free speech, did not ban the film but did censor one sequence of the film. A new Massachusetts state law authorizing censorship was passed. Working with the national office, other NAACP chapters succeeded in getting the film censored or banned altogether.

NAACP chapters were also organized in Chicago, Philadelphia, and Washington, D.C. In the nation's capital, segregation and discrimination in federal government jobs were severely limiting opportunities for advancement for blacks and, even worse, reducing the number of jobs available to blacks. This situation served as a rallying point for organizing a Washington chapter.

In a report to the 1914 NAACP annual meeting, Archibald H. Grimke, the Washington chapter president, said, "Segregation was the thing that did the work for us. The people became aroused and began to look around for the instrument that could help them. We took great pains to point out that there is only one organization in this country that can do this work and that is the National Association for the Advancement of Colored People. I called the attention of our Washington people to the fact that it is of the utmost importance that we assist such an organization in its work."[7] By the end of 1913, the Washington chapter boasted a membership of four hundred and had raised $3,000 to support the work of the national office.

In 1912, the NAACP had eleven branches and a total of 1,100 members. The national office staff took to the road to encourage the organization of more branches. In midwestern cities they encountered a number of problems. In Columbus, Ohio, a local branch of black men was divided by jealousy and rivalry. In Springfield, Ohio, a group of black ministers could not get white support. In Omaha, a white man tried to take over the chapter. In Detroit, women were not admitted to the branch, while in Indianapolis, the branch membership was entirely female and Indianapolis men were organizing their own branch. The NAACP staff members dealt with these problems and managed to work most of them out.

Booker T. Washington died in 1915, and afterward, NAACP members took time off from organization-building to heal an old wound. During his life, Washington headed a faction that opposed and obstructed many of the efforts of the NAACP. In November 1916, the Amenia Conference was held at the estate of NAACP chairman Joel Spingarn, with the goal of bringing the two factions together. The group of fifty attendees drew up resolutions calling for education and political freedom for blacks and pledged to forget past controversies and suspicions and work together. Considering the strong feelings on both sides, the conference was an event of remarkable unanimity. The black newspaper *The New York Age* wrote that the conference "marked the birth of a new spirit of united purpose and effort."[8]

One speaker at the conference was James Weldon Johnson, a noted black writer. His contribution to the unity and harmony of the conference caught Spingarn's eye. The chairman of the board felt that Johnson would make an excellent field secretary, whose duties would be to oversee branches and organize new ones. Spingarn invited Johnson to join the NAACP staff. In considering the offer, Johnson saw his experience as a teacher, editor, and writer as preparation and prelude for such work with the NAACP. He joined the staff in December 1916.

As he approached his task of organizing branches, Johnson found that sixty-eight of the branches were in northern and western cities, while only three were in the South. The challenge was clearly in the South. Some members of the board feared that southern branches, located as they would be in the heartland of racial bigotry, would cause the organization, out of fear of reprisals to southern branches, to soften its fearless stand for equality for blacks. These officials also thought that involving southern blacks in the work would expose them to violence and other forms of reprisals from whites.

Johnson felt that southern chapters, which would probably be mostly black, would bring large numbers of black people into the effort. He believed that "the organization could not reach its goals by hammering at white America," that "it would be necessary to awaken black America to a sense of its rights" and that "the ultimate and vital part of the work would have to be done by black America itself."[9]

Johnson won over the majority of the board and began his project. He prepared a manual for branches that described the goals of the NAACP bylaws and a plan for forming a branch. Letters went out to leading citizens in twenty southern cities asking each to form a group of twenty-five people who would schedule a meeting with Johnson. In January 1917, he set out to meet with the twenty groups in southern cities from Richmond, Virginia, to Tampa, Florida. At nineteen of the cities, branches were organized. The foundation was laid for what the NAACP would come to call its southern empire.

By 1919, there were 310 branches, 131 of them in the South. In April 1918, in honor of the seventieth birthday of its first president, Morefield Storey, the NAACP launched a nationwide membership drive. Membership was nearly ten thousand at that point. The goal of the drive was to increase membership to fifty thousand. By June 1919, membership was over fifty-six thousand.

At its tenth-anniversary meeting, the NAACP proudly called itself "the greatest fighting force for Negro freedom in the world. The Negro who is not a member finds himself on the defensive. The white man who does not believe in it does not believe in American democracy."[10]

In those early years, nothing seemed more pressing to that "fighting force" than fighting the evil of lynching.

IV

THE CAMPAIGN AGAINST LYNCHING

The cover of the postcard depicts a group of white men gathered proudly around their quarry. Their quarry is a black man whom they have just brutally beaten and killed—a lynching victim. The message on the other side of the card reads: "This is the way we do them down here. Will put you on our regular mailing list. Expect one a month on the average." The card bears the postmark of a small Alabama town and was sent in December 1911 to Reverend John H. Holmes, pastor of the Unitarian Church in New York City. It was a defiant response to a speech attacking lynching that Holmes had recently given at an NAACP-sponsored meeting. The photo clearly depicted the faces of the white men. They could easily have been identified as implicated in a lynching. "The men's confidence that no one would dream of prosecuting them was the most striking thing about the card. We wondered that it had been permitted to go through the U.S. Mail," said Mary Ovington.[1]

A race riot had inspired the formation of the

NAACP. Now the brazen lawlessness of the postcard inspired something akin to an NAACP battle plan. A map of the United States was posted in the office with pins marking every site of a lynching. "The lower part of the map was black with pinheads," noted Ovington.[2]

The country needed to know about the brutality of lynching. Through *The Crisis,* pamphlets, and meetings, the NAACP put pressure on the public to deplore and fight lynching. *The Crisis* published the annual toll: one hundred lynchings in 1911, sixty-three in 1912, seventy-nine in 1913. Pamphlets were mailed out describing the details of particular lynchings and the lack of effort by law enforcement officials to apprehend and bring the lynchers to justice. NAACP staff members, black and white, traveled to the scenes of many lynchings to investigate and bring back details for publication. These details were also used by NAACP lawyers to pursue the conviction of lynchers.

In May 1911, a particularly brutal lynching took place in Livermore, Kentucky. A black man charged with the murder of a white man was taken to an opera house and strung up in the center of the stage. Admission fees were charged to those who wished to watch him die. Those in the orchestra seats were allowed to empty their revolvers into the black man while those in the gallery were allowed one shot.

The NAACP executive committee, shocked and appalled by this lynching, sent appeals to President William Howard Taft, to the vice president, to the speaker of the House of Representatives, and to the chairmen of the judiciary committees of the House and Senate. The contents of the appeal calling for action against "the foul blot and the intolerable conditions of law by lynching" were also provided to the Associated Press and selected newspapers. A committee of ten personally delivered the appeal to the president. President Taft said that there was nothing he could do—that the individual states had to deal with the problem. Oswald Villard, chairman of the NAACP executive committee, wrote to the governor of Kentucky but got no response.

In 1912, Albert E. Pillsbury, a former attorney general of Massachusetts and a member of the NAACP executive committee, wrote in the *Harvard Law Review*, "The United States has, as all governments have, a political and legal interest in the lives of its citizens. If it has not full power to protect them it is only because that duty rests solely upon the states. . . . [I]t is a duty owed to the United States, as well as to the individual citizens. . . . [O]pen and notorious neglect or omission of this duty on the part of a state by allowing mobs to murder citizens is an offense against the nation for which the United States has the right to exact punishment." Pillsbury ended his article by calling for an antilynching law which could then be tested by the courts for its constitutionality.[3]

But appeals and law review articles didn't help southern black families, who lived everyday with the fear of lynching. Many packed up and headed north. By 1915, disasters, such as floods, and the promise of jobs in the North had pushed the migration north to a new high. In 1917, after visiting six states, DuBois estimated that since the turn of the century, 250,000 black people had left the South.

Many NAACP members felt that leaving the South and moving to the less oppressive North was one solution for blacks. Others wondered whether blacks' problems would simply be transplanted; they proved to be correct. Moving north, black migrants often couldn't find jobs. Many blacks, jobless or working at menial, low-paying jobs, crowded into slums, where crime and violence often developed. This situation led to increased prejudice and racial unrest in many northern cities.

Such a situation came to a head in East St. Louis, Illinois, a heavily industrial city where stockyards, meat-packing plants, and a major railroad junction provided many menial jobs. Many employers were fighting unionization by hiring blacks. Black community leaders had been accused of bringing blacks from the South to vote Republican in the 1916 election; in those days, most blacks voted "the party of Lincoln." Racial feelings ran high as the summer of 1917 came to East St. Louis.

A riot broke out in the city on July 2. Hundreds of blacks were killed or injured. Black homes were burned to the ground, leaving six thousand blacks homeless. At a congressional hearing, Missouri congressman Leonides Dyer reported on an interview with an army lieutenant. "He saw members of the militia shoot negroes. He saw East St. Louis policemen shoot negroes. He saw mobs go to the homes of these negroes and nail boards over the doors and windows and then set fire and burn them up. He saw them take little children out of the arms of their mothers and throw them into the fires."[4] Nevertheless, blacks were held responsible for the riot, and many were arrested. The NAACP raised money for their defense and for relief for those left homeless by the riot.

But the NAACP felt that something more needed to be done to tell the world that the East St. Louis massacre was a terrible wrong that must never happen again. On July 28, ten thousand black men, women, and children stepped out to the beat of muffled drums in a silent protest parade down New York City's Fifth Avenue. The men wore black; the women and children wore white. Some carried banners that read "Give Me a Chance to Live," "Treat Us So That We May Love Our Country," "Mother, Do Lynchers Go to Heaven?" Several men leading the march carried a banner that read "Your Hands Are Full of Blood." Many of those lining the street watching the silent marchers were in tears.

As the marchers passed by, black Boy Scouts handed out flyers that expressed the thoughts of the silent marchers. "We march because by the grace of God and the force of truth, the dangerous hampering walls of prejudice and inhuman injustices must fall . . . because we want to make impossible a repetition of . . . East St. Louis by rousing the conscience of the country and bringing the murderers of our brothers, sisters, and innocent children to justice. . . . [W]e deem it a crime to be silent in the face of such barbaric acts. . . . [W]e want our children to live in a better land and enjoy fairer conditions than have fallen our lot."[5]

As he marched silently down Fifth Avenue, James Weldon Johnson was thinking of his fellow marchers and those people who watched from the curb. Both could be harmed by the brutality of lynching and riots. This insight came to him a month before, when he went to Memphis to investigate the lynching of a black man accused of being an ax murderer. After talking to the sheriff, newspaper reporters, and white and black citizens, he could find no good evidence that the man was guilty. The man had not had a trial. A mob had taken him from jail and burned him alive.

As Johnson visited the lynching site, marked by a pile of ashes— most of the bones had been taken for souvenirs—he thought of the scene as it had been described to him. The man is chained to a stake. Wood is piled around him. Gasoline is poured on him. He is set afire. Five thousand people, some with children in their arms, gather around to watch the man's agony. It is over, and as the crowd breaks up, someone says, "They burned him too fast."[6]

It occurred to Johnson that those who watched were morally damaged by the experience. He would later write, "Estimate if you can the effect upon the making of the character of the American people caused by the opportunity ... to practice injustice, wrong, and brutality for 300 years with impunity upon a practically defenseless minority." Johnson came to see that the race question involved the saving of black America's body and white America's soul.[7]

As the NAACP campaign to press state officials to act against lynching proceeded, NAACP officials were seeing small victories here and there.

– In 1911, the Alabama Supreme Court rendered a decision that resulted in the firing of a sheriff who had allowed the lynching of a black prisoner.
– In 1912, the governor of Pennsylvania recommended that the town of Coatesville lose its charter because it had been protecting lynchers. The lynchers had taken a black man, accused of killing a policeman in a fight, from a hospital and burned him alive.
– In 1916, an Ohio sheriff kept a mob at bay that was intent on seizing a black prisoner.
– In Kentucky in 1917, the governor himself stood up to a mob attempting to take a black prisoner.
– In 1918, a Tennessee law-and-order group was formed to stop lynching.
– The governor of North Carolina asked for and got 250 federal soldiers to protect a black prisoner. Fifteen members of the mob were convicted and sentenced to jail.

While this news was encouraging, the NAACP wanted to see such things happening across the land. And no one could send as strong a message as the president of the United States. Following a particularly brutal lynching of a black man in Tennessee in 1918, the NAACP sent a protest to President Woodrow Wilson. The response came from the attorney general, who said, quite implausibly, that the nation was at war (World War I), and the government had no jurisdiction because the crime had nothing to do with the war effort![8]

The NAACP sent more appeals to the president, but none actually reached his desk. Not until James Weldon Johnson mentioned the appeal during a meeting with Wilson did the president learn of the appeals. Wilson promised to "seek an opportunity" to urge the nation to put a stop to lynching.

The pressure on the president was increased when forty-four NAACP chapters were contacted and asked to write or wire the president to condemn lynching in his Fourth of July speech. One chapter succeeded in persuading the governor of West Virginia and two West Virginia Supreme Court judges, as well as other influential white and black citizens, to send telegrams. But Wilson did not mention the matter on Independence Day.

Finally, in a public statement on July 26, Wilson asked officials and citizens to bring an end to lynching, which cannot "live where the community does not endorse it." Jubilantly, the NAACP printed and distributed fifty thousand copies of the statement.

In the midst of its antilynching campaign, the NAACP had to turn its attention to finding a new leader for the national office. In 1918, the national office was without an executive secretary. The last one, Roy Nash, had left to fight in World War I. The leaderless office was being run by those who could give only part of their time to the effort. The board decided it was time to hire an experienced administrator. John Shillady, a white man who had had a great deal of experience in administering social service agencies, was hired in April 1918 as executive secretary. Also joining the organization at that time as assistant secretary was Walter White, recruited from the Atlanta branch by James Weldon Johnson. Just one year out of Atlanta University, White was working for an insurance company. Because White, who had a black heritage, was blond and blue-eyed, he was sometimes called a volunteer Negro. His appearance would serve him well in his first assignment, that of investigating lynchings.

One of Shillady's first acts was to assign two staff members to research the lynchings that had taken place from 1889 to the current year—1918. Working in the Library of Congress, the researchers looked through the previous thirty years of newspapers. Notes were compiled on the name, sex, and age of the victim, on the place, date, and other details of the lynching, and on the reason for the lynching. While accusations of rape and murder topped the list of reasons, others were such things as talking back or not getting off the road to let a white person pass. Ten states had had more than one hundred lynchings, with Georgia leading the list with 386.[9]

In 1919, the NAACP published the data, which included narratives of one hundred carefully investigated lynchings, in a book titled *Thirty Years of Lynching in the United States, 1889–1918*. The book, distributed to newspapers, public officials, and other opinion leaders, provided a tragic toll of 3,224 people lynched in the thirty years since 1889. Even so, the NAACP believed that its numbers were low. Occasionally, unidentified disfigured black bodies were found floating down a stream or in the woods. Often the family of a lynch victim had fled in fear, and no one was left to identify the body. Cases such as these usually weren't written up in the newspapers.

In an effort to get major newspaper coverage of the horror of lynching, the NAACP convened an Anti-Lynching Conference in May 1919. The call for the meeting went out over the signatures of the U.S attorney general, former secretary of state Elihu Root, former chief justice Charles Evans Hughes, three former governors, and seventeen prominent southerners. Twenty-five hundred people attended, and they adopted three resolutions calling for an effort to get federal and state antilynch laws passed and to continue the antilynching advertising. Following the conference, "An Address to the Nation on Lynching" was written and signed by those people who issued the call, as well as by former president William Howard Taft, the president of Princeton University, the governor of Tennessee, and an Episcopal bishop from Mississippi. This document, which called for an antilynch law, was used to pressure Congress to investigate the problem.

In 1919, aware of a rise in racial tension in the South, the NAACP sent a representative to several southern states to investigate the reasons. He talked to whites and blacks alike and found a great deal of concern among whites about the blacks' rising status as a result of having served in the army during the war. Most whites considered blacks inferior and not fit to enjoy political, economic, and social equality, and politicians and newspapers encouraged these feelings. One candidate running for the Louisiana legislature said during his campaign speeches that lynching was necessary and that education made black males into confident men and black women into prostitutes. Some southerners believed that a federal antilynch law was the way to fight the problem, while some southern whites said they would defy such a law to protect white women from black men. One black leader offered an ominous warning: blacks were arming themselves, and only federal action would forestall violence.

Violence did indeed come. Small incidents, fanned by the attitudes producing the racial tensions found by the NAACP investigator, erupted into riots.

In June 1919, in Longview, Texas, many whites and blacks were killed in a riot involving returning black and white soldiers. This riot marked the beginning of what would come to be known as Red Summer. Race riots broke out in twenty-six cities, including Chicago, Omaha, Knoxville, Indianapolis, and Washington. The Washington riot lasted three days. These riots were actually small wars, for blacks were fighting back with weapons. Some blacks were lynched simply because of statements they made that whites felt would incite a riot. In all, seventy-nine blacks were lynched during Red Summer.

In the midst of the bloody summer, John Shillady went to Austin, Texas, to meet with state officials, who out of fear of the new black militancy wanted to ban NAACP branches in Texas. While there, Shillady was beaten into unconsciousness by a group of white men that included a constable and a county judge. Once he had received medical care for his injuries, Shillady took the first train to New York. An Associated Press reporter was on the train and filed a story headlined "Shillady Beaten Up at Austin, Texas." By the time Shillady got back to New York, everyone knew what had happened to him. He was greeted at New York's Pennsylvania Station by dozens of black Red Caps running down the platform shouting "Shillady! Shillady!" He was their hero. He had suffered for them.

Shillady had suffered more than bruises and cuts in the beating. He had seen the cruelty of bigotry, felt its physical and emotional pain. His spirit was broken. He did not believe that such cruelty could be overcome by people such as himself who believed in law and order. Mary Ovington described him as shell-shocked.[10] Once a cheery, confident man, Shillady became sad and indecisive. He resigned the post of executive secretary a few months later with the words "I am less confident . . . of the probability of overcoming the forces opposed to Negro equality by the means and methods which are within the Association's power to employ." He was in and out of the hospital after his resignation and died shortly thereafter.[11]

James Weldon Johnson was selected to take Shillady's place, becoming, in 1919, the NAACP's first black executive secretary. His was the job of picking up the pieces of an office in disarray as a result of Shillady's months of inactivity.

Almost at once, the association faced a new challenge. A group of black farmers in Phillips County, Arkansas, had decided to join together in an effort to get a better price for their cotton crop. During a meeting they were attacked and fired upon by a group of whites, who charged that the blacks were planning to take over the country. The blacks returned the fire. Whites and blacks were killed in the battle. Groups of whites scoured the surrounding countryside, shooting every black they encountered. Many black families fled the county. Blacks who stayed were herded into fenced-in areas. Those who swore they had nothing to do with the farmers' organization and promised to work without pay for a certain amount of time were allowed to leave. Seventy-nine men would not give in. They were put on trial for murder and insurrection. Armed men attended the trial, listening intently and interrupting the proceedings frequently to threaten the judge and the jury. Twelve of the accused black men were sentenced to death; the rest received prison sentences.

The NAACP organized a defense for the men. Scipio Jones, a black Little Rock lawyer, handled the case in Arkansas. After five years of trials in the Arkansas courts and two hearings in the U.S. Supreme Court, the NAACP won the freedom of all seventy-nine men. The high court overturned the Arkansas verdict on the grounds that the judge and jury were dominated by armed men. The victory had great legal significance. Blacks and whites could not legally be lynched.

Late in 1919, Johnson began the effort to get a federal antilynch law enacted. He met with Missouri Congressman Leonides Dyer, one legislator who in the past had tried to get such a law passed. Dyer said he believed it could be done. Johnson promised to lobby the House Judiciary Committee, which would have to approve the bill before it could go to the floor for a vote. The bill, introduced by Dyer in April 1921, assured persons within the jurisdiction of every state the equal protection of the laws and set forth punishment for the crime of lynching. The bill went to the Judiciary Committee, and Johnson began two years of lobbying, trudging the halls of Congress day after day, talking to senators and representatives, trying to win their support.

The bill emerged from committee on October 20, 1921. The next step was to get the bill placed on the docket for prompt consideration. This required more lobbying for Johnson—more phone calls, more meetings with members of Congress. He contacted the NAACP office in New York and asked the staff to get the branches to send letters to members of Congress.

Finally, the bill was to be brought up for consideration by the House of Representatives. Many influential and not-so-influential people flooded the offices of congressmen with copies of editorials, letters, telegrams, and phone calls, all urging that the bill be passed.

Debate on the bill began January 25, 1922. Representatives from Mississippi and Texas argued that the federal government could do nothing about mob rule. They said that lynching was caused by the rape of white women and that in such cases the white community went mad and acted according to a "higher law—

the defense of white womanhood."[12] But Johnson had supplied the supporters of the bill with statistics showing that in the past thirty-three years less than 17 percent of lynch victims had been accused of rape—and that sixty-four black women had been lynched. The supporters of the bill used these figures in their speeches.

The word that the antilynch bill was being debated spread quickly through the black community, and blacks jammed the House gallery to hear the proceedings. As supporters made a telling point, blacks, in complete violation of the rules, stood and cheered. On the second day, the bill passed, 230 to 119.

Black people across the country were jubilant, but the battle was only half won. Johnson knew that getting the bill passed by the Senate would not be a two-day feat. Many of the senators were constitutional lawyers for whom the constitutionality of the bill was an issue. Did the Constitution give the federal government the power to ban lynching? Lynching was murder, and like murder, shouldn't its punishment be left to the states? Those were the questions they wanted answered. While the Supreme Court could rule on this matter once the bill was a law, the senators believed they must resolve the question before it became a law.

For two weeks, the bill hung in the Senate Judiciary Committee. The NAACP pressed the Senate to enact the law. A petition signed by twenty-four state governors, thirty-nine mayors, forty-seven judges and lawyers, eighty-eight bishops, twenty-nine college presidents, and thirty editors, as well as by other influential Americans, was sent to the Senate.

Finally, in June 1922, the committee held hearings. Johnson testified, and in his presentation he provided an argument supporting the constitutionality of the law. "It is not only against the act of killing that the federal government seeks to exercise its power through the proposed law, but against the act of the mob in abrogating to itself the functions of the state and substituting its actions for the due processes of law guaranteed by the Constitution to every person accused of crime."[13] Johnson labeled lynching "anarchy—anarchy which the states have proven themselves powerless to cope with."[14]

The bill was introduced to the Senate floor on September 21. Democratic senators blocked voting on the bill by stalling and filibustering. Leaving the chamber without a quorum (enough senators to call for a vote), raising inconsequential points of order, and making long-winded speeches about almost anything at all served to stall the call for a vote. Republican supporters of the bill did little to counteract the filibuster. The filibuster paralyzed the Senate until December 2, when the Republicans abandoned their support of the bill so that other Senate business could be transacted.

Johnson felt betrayed by the Republican senators whom he had worked with for months. He felt that they had given the bill token support and let the Democrats take the blame for killing it.

The Dyer antilynch bill did not become law, but Johnson said "it made the floors of Congress a forum in which facts were discussed and brought home to the American people as they never had before. . . . [T]he debate was one of the prime factors in reducing the number of lynchings in the decade that followed to less than one-third of what it had been in the preceding decade. . . . [I]t served to awaken the people of the southern states to the necessity of taking steps themselves to wipe out the crime."[15]

In the years to come, Walter White, who succeeded Johnson as executive secretary, made two more efforts to get antilynch laws passed. Both the Costigan-Wagner bill (1931) and the Wagner-Gavagan bill

(1940) were passed by the House but fell victim to fili-busters in the Senate.

Congress never did pass an antilynching bill. How-ever, the activity to support the bills stimulated the growth of the NAACP branches, brought in increased donations, and made the organization the acknowl-edged leader and speaker for blacks and civil rights. The NAACP's campaign of antilynch law lobbying and publicity portraying the brutality of lynching, the trumped-up charges against the victim, and the obvi-ous threat to law and order served to turn public opin-ion against lynching so that, by the 1950s, lynching had virtually ended. Violence against blacks, however, has not disappeared, but today such violence, whether by private individuals or by agents of the government, like police, is much more likely to bring down upon the instigators the full force of the justice system.

V

GETTING THE VOTE

"The right of the citizens of the United States to vote shall not be denied or abridged by the United States or by any state on account of race, color, or previous condition of servitude." The words of the Fifteenth Amendment to the Constitution gave black people the right to vote in 1870. Yet in 1910, most of the 9 million black Americans living in the South could not vote. Why weren't they voting? Southern states were placing a variety of legal obstacles in the path of the would-be black voter, and the Supreme Court was upholding these obstacles with its decisions.

Getting the vote for blacks was the topic of the second NAACP conference, held in May 1910 in New York City. Speakers discussed such topics as voting for candidates who would work for the cause of black people rather than for the party candidate. They talked about disfranchisement (being denied the vote) and how it robbed blacks of the right to control the quality of public education for their children. DuBois called disfranchisement "a major barrier to Negro advancement."[1] The conference concluded with a resolution that the NAACP focus on working for voting rights for black people. Thus began an NAACP campaign to fight the many devious ways that states resorted to in order to keep blacks from voting.

By 1910, Oklahoma, as well as several other southern states, had added a grandfather clause amendment to its constitution, which required that voters be able to read and write. But a person would be exempted from this rule if an ancestor had voted before 1866. The Oklahoma legislature believed that since race was not mentioned, there was no violation of the Fifteenth Amendment. But NAACP's president, Morefield Storey, a former president of the American Bar Association, believed that the amendment did violate the Fifteenth Amendment. Storey convinced the U.S. solicitor general to challenge the Oklahoma amendment before the Supreme Court. The solicitor general presented the case of *Guinn* v. *United States* before the Supreme Court and invited Storey to take part in the argument. In June 1915, the Supreme Court found that while the Oklahoma amendment did not deny the vote, its effect was a violation of the Fifteenth Amendment.

This was the NAACP's first Supreme Court victory. The result was that southern states abandoned the tactic of the grandfather clause. But they were determined to deny the vote to black people.

Oklahoma legislators passed a new amendment, which said that those already registered would remain qualified voters but that new voters had twelve days in which to register or be forever barred from voting. The NAACP contested this new amendment before the Supreme Court, which declared it, too, in violation of the Fifteenth Amendment.

In 1923, Texas legislators thought they had found a substitute for the grandfather clause. They passed a law that blacks could not vote in primaries. In the solidly Democratic south, not being allowed to vote in the primary was to be denied the vote. Before NAACP lawyers could challenge the law in court, they needed a test case—some brave Texan had to risk the wrath of the Klan and try to vote in the primary. They found such a brave man in the person of Dr. L. A. Nixon of El Paso. Nixon had become a leader in opposing black disfranchisement. Despite pleas from his family and friends, Nixon attempted to vote in the Democratic primary. He was refused but not physically harmed.

Nixon sued the El Paso election officials who would not let him vote in the primary. The lower court dismissed his case. The NAACP appealed the lower court's action before the Supreme Court. On March 7, 1927, the Court upheld Nixon's right to vote in the Democratic primary. In the decision, Justice Oliver Wendell Holmes wrote, "The statute of Texas . . . assumes to forbid negroes to take part in a primary election . . . discriminating against them by the distinction of color alone. . . . [I]t is too clear for extended argument that color cannot be made the basis of a statutory classification affecting the right setup in this case."[2]

The high court's decision was clear. Using the primary tactic would not work for those who would deny the ballot to blacks. But Texas governor Dan Moody wouldn't hear of it: blacks would not vote in Texas. Texas lawmakers proceeded to pass a law that gave the Democratic executive committee the authority to set primary voting rules. Right after the legislative session, the Democratic committee passed a resolution that "all white Democrats who are qualified under the Constitution and laws of Texas and none others are allowed to participate in the primary elections." The Supreme Court ruled against this law in 1932.[3]

Undaunted, Texas and seven other southern states

passed laws giving those delegates attending the Democratic convention the right to make primary voting rules. When the convention met, the delegates voted to exclude blacks from voting in primaries. Once more the question of voting in a primary would have to be argued before the Supreme Court. In 1941, when Dr. Lonnie Smith of Houston was not allowed to vote in the primary, he called on the NAACP for help. NAACP lawyers pleaded Smith's suit for the right to vote in the primaries in two lower courts. When both courts ruled against Smith, the NAACP appealed to the Supreme Court. In 1944, in *Smith* v. *Allwright,* the Supreme Court ruled that "it may be taken as a postulate that the right to vote in such a primary for the nomination of candidates without discrimination by the state, like the right to vote in a general election is a right secured by the Constitution."[4]

By 1946, most southern states had bowed to the law of the land, and blacks were allowed to vote in primary and general elections. Still, a few states continued to look for ways to bar blacks from the polls. Among these states, South Carolina was the most determined. When blacks were denied the opportunity to vote in the South Carolina primary in 1946, the NAACP went to the U.S. District Court, where Judge J. Waties Waring upheld the right of blacks to vote in primaries. "It is time for South Carolina to rejoin the Union. It is time to fall in step with the other states and to adopt the American way of conducting elections," he ruled.[5]

Even as the NAACP was pursuing the legal battle for the vote, it was also reaping the fruit of its labors—political power. In 1930, President Herbert Hoover nominated North Carolina's Judge John J. Parker to a vacancy on the Supreme Court. The nomination was intended to reward the voters of North Carolina who had helped elect Hoover to the presidency. Parker was not well known, but the NAACP decided to investigate his record with respect to blacks. It was discovered that, while running in the 1920 North Carolina gubernatorial election, Parker had publicly announced his approval of the poll tax, literacy tests for voters, and the grandfather clause that had been declared unconstitutional by the Supreme Court in 1915. He was quoted in the Greensboro *Daily Times* as having said, "The participation of the Negro in politics is a source of evil and danger to both races and is not desired by the wise man in either race or by the Republican party of North Carolina."[6]

Did Parker say what the newspaper quoted him as saying, and if so, did he still hold such opinions in 1930? The NAACP sent him a telegram with these concerns and asked Western Union to confirm delivery of the message. Western Union confirmed that the telegram had been delivered to Parker personally. Seventy-two hours passed, and Parker had not yet replied.

Walter White, the acting executive secretary of the NAACP, asked President Hoover to withdraw the Parker nomination. The president angrily refused. The nomination was being considered by the Senate Judiciary Committee, which had formed a subcommittee to hold hearings. White presented the NAACP's position to the subcommittee. Parker, White said, had advocated the disfranchisement of black American citizens, despite the explicit provisions of the Fourteenth and Fifteenth amendments—certainly not appropriate for a Supreme Court justice. Representatives of organized labor, which opposed Parker because he had upheld labor contracts they considered unfavorable, also testified at the hearing.

NAACP headquarters wired all of its branches, urging members to send telegrams of protest to their senators. NAACP members, in turn, recruited member churches, fraternal, civic, educational, and other organizations to contact their senators. The NAACP held mass meetings and supplied telegraph forms to those who attended. Senators were besieged with telegrams, letters, petitions, and phone calls—all protesting Parker's appointment. At first angered, then surprised, the senators began to grasp the groundswell of black opinion that had come down on them. The subcommittee voted 10 to 6 against confirmation.

President Hoover would not have it. He forced the nomination onto the Senate floor for a vote. Blacks kept up the pressure on their senators. Opposing the Parker nomination became the talk of the black community. Everyone, from doctors to teachers to waiters, was contacting their senators.

On May 7, the day of the vote, black people crowded into the Senate gallery. White kept track of the "aye" and "nay" votes as the clerk called the roll. As White did his final tally, it looked as if they had won. Could he be wrong? He checked his numbers again. Then came the clerk's announcement: 39 for confirmation, 41 against. They had won. Blacks had pulled together and achieved a significant political victory. Southern newspapers mourned for a nation in which black people dictated to the president and the Senate, but northern newspapers praised the effort as a "coming of age" for black voters.

The NAACP then proceeded to put the ballot to work to reelect its Senate supporters and defeat senators who had voted to confirm Parker. *The Crisis* published the names of the senators who had voted for Parker. "The following Senators have Negro constituents . . . and against the express wishes of these constituents they voted for the confirmation of Judge Parker. . . . Paste this in your hat and keep it there."[7]

For the next several years, the NAACP marshaled black voters to defeat those senators who had voted to confirm Parker. In Ohio, New Jersey, Kansas, California, Maryland, Indiana, Pennsylvania, West Virginia, Connecticut, and Rhode Island, senators were defeated thanks mainly to blacks who had not forgotten what happened that May day in the Senate chamber. Two senators who voted against Parker were reelected.

By 1944, a careful look at black voter rolls showed that black voters outnumbered white voters in seventeen states. The political conventions to nominate presidential candidates were coming up for that summer. The nation was involved in World War II. Black service people were helping to win freedom from fascism for Europeans and Asians. The irony of their second-class citizenship in their own country needed to be addressed. Representatives of twenty-five leading black organizations, including the NAACP, met in New York to discuss ways to use black voting power to influence the upcoming political campaigns to deal with issues important to black people. The organization representatives wrote a statement for presentation to the platform committees of both parties. The statement called for full citizenship for blacks—the elimination of the poll tax, the passage of an antilynch law, the desegregation of the armed forces, and the establishment of a federal committee on fair employment practices. Noting the past political victories of black voters in the Parker case and in senatorial elections, the statement pointed out that "negroes no longer belong to any one political party. They will vote for men and measures."[8]

The Republicans did include in their platform a call for a Fair Employment Practice Commission and some mild criticism of black disfranchisement and lynching. But the effort to include in the platforms issues important to blacks essentially failed.

As World War II ended, black servicemen returned with high expectations for democracy in their country but were met instead with discrimination and violence. The NAACP organized a committee of black leaders and churchmen, who met with President Harry Truman to talk about the continued violation of the civil rights of black Americans. The president appointed a commission to investigate the situation.

Black people had found a firm advocate in the person of President Truman. In June 1947, he addressed the NAACP national convention, calling for federal, state, and individual action against lynching, disfranchisement, the poll tax, educational and employment inequality, and all of the discriminatory methods used to degrade and impede black people. Four major radio networks carried his speech, and the State Department arranged to have it broadcast worldwide by short wave. Several million people heard the president of the United States forthrightly promise to end the violation of the black person's civil rights. Truman said, in part, "We can no longer afford the luxury of a leisurely attack upon prejudice and discrimination. There is much that state and local governments can do in providing positive safeguards for civil rights. But we cannot any longer, await the growth of a will to action in the slowest state or the most backward community. Our national government must show the way."[9]

As he finished his speech and stepped away from the podium, Truman turned to Walter White and said, "I mean every word of it and I am going to prove that I do mean it."

By late 1947, the President's Commission on Civil Rights had produced a document called *To Secure These Rights* that spelled out an extensive program for securing and protecting the civil rights of black people. In a special address to Congress, Truman presented the commission's program, which included provisions for protecting blacks' right to vote.

For the next two decades, *To Secure These Rights*

would be the NAACP's blueprint for achieving the rights of blacks. The NAACP decided that a strong lobbying group should be formed to press for implementation of this blueprint. In fall 1949, the NAACP convened the National Emergency Civil Rights Mobilization, inviting lobbying groups from unions, trade associations, churches, civil rights groups, and black organizations. Altogether, four thousand people from thirty-five states attended the meeting, which was held in Washington, D.C.

The attendees formed the Leadership Conference on Civil Rights, which would function as a coordinating organization for 130 civil rights, labor, business, religious, civic, and fraternal organizations. The goal of the conference was to work toward the passage and enforcement of civil rights legislation. Members were to meet with senators, congressional people, and the president in a continuous lobbying effort for civil rights.

By 1957, the Leadership Conference had managed to influence Congress to begin to act on the blueprint. Congress passed the Civil Rights Act of 1957, which established the U.S. Commission on Civil Rights and made it a federal crime to interfere with a citizen's right to vote.

The 1957 Civil Rights Act was the first civil rights act passed since the Act of 1875. But that Act and the Civil Rights Act of 1960, which called for federal supervision of voter registration, both failed to provide for enforcement of the right of blacks to vote. The Leadership Conference had been involved in helping to write both acts but could do little when Congress refused to retain sections that gave the attorney general the power to correct abuses of blacks' constitutional rights.

In the early 1960s, college students, many of them NAACP members, moved in to help blacks in the

South register to vote. They served as advisors and escorts for blacks. At this point, faced with the strong civil rights laws being passed, whites determined to stop blacks from voting had little to resort to but violence. For the most part they directed their violence against the college students, killing and injuring some of them. Nevertheless, this voter registration effort resulted in the registration of seven hundred thousand black voters in the South.

The NAACP-led Leadership Conference continued to press for a stronger law. In 1964, another Civil Rights Act was passed, this one a far-reaching law that addressed many areas of discrimination and segregation, including a stronger measure guaranteeing the right of the black voter to register. The NAACP mounted another drive to register black voters. By the 1964 presidential election, the U.S. voter rolls boasted six million black voters.

In the wake of the enthusiasm that followed the passage of the 1964 Act, Congress moved quickly to approve other measures that helped to protect the right of blacks to vote. One such measure, passed in 1964, was the Twenty-Fourth Amendment to the Constitution, which abolished the poll tax. Since the early 1900s, the poll tax had been one of the most common methods of disfranchising black people. For years, the NAACP had worked to have an anti-poll-tax law passed, but Congress had never acted because interfering with a state tax was thought to be unconstitutional. Now the illegality of the poll tax had become a part of the Constitution.

At this point, President Lyndon Johnson was taking the lead, calling NAACP executive secretary Roy Wilkins to describe the next civil rights bill he would present to Congress. The Civil Rights Act of 1965 swiftly followed. The act dealt with all of the devices used to keep blacks from voting—outlawing the difficult oral and written exams, literacy tests, character references, and the many other devices used by registrars. With the acceleration of the NAACP voter registration drive, the Act had an almost immediate effect. In Arkansas, Alabama, Mississippi, and South Carolina, the NAACP helped eighty-four thousand black voters register. As federal examiners, provided for by the 1965 Act, moved in to supervise registration, 350,000 more black voters were registered. The number of black voters on the voting rolls in the South began to rise. By 1968, more than 50 percent of all eligible blacks were registered. Blacks began to put their candidates into office. By 1969, 1,200 blacks had been elected to public office. By the 1990s, over seven thousand black men and women held political office.

Today, many blacks hold prominent political office —most large cities are headed by black mayors. There is one black governor. And Democrats and Republicans have serious political discussions about running a black candidate for vice president. With state-mandated impediments for voting abolished, the task now is to get blacks out to vote—a task being addressed by periodic NAACP voter registration drives.

VI

FIGHTING THE CASTE OF COLOR IN TRANSPORTATION AND HOUSING

At the beginning of the twentieth century, segregation laws governed every aspect of life in America, particularly in the South. Use of public facilities was restricted for, or forbidden to, blacks. They had to enter banks, city buildings, and theaters through the back door. Blacks could not stay in hotels, eat in restaurants, or shop in many department stores. They were restricted to "colored" sections on buses and trains and in theaters, cemeteries, and residential areas. Black children attended separate "colored" schools.

This pervasive caste of color that kept blacks separate from whites in virtually every aspect of life had its roots in the master–slave customs of slavery. Such separation from whites delivered a message to blacks that they were an inferior caste, not good enough to mingle with whites. Here and there states had been bold enough to pass segregation laws. Then, in the 1890s, a significant Supreme Court decision paved the way for hundreds of segregation laws. Homer Plessy, a black man, defied an 1890 Louisiana segregation law that called for trains to provide "equal but separate accommodations for the white and colored races" by taking a seat in the white section of a train for a trip from New Orleans to Covington, Louisiana. He was arrested for violating the state law and found guilty in a Louisiana court. Plessy eventually appealed the verdict to the Supreme Court, charging Louisiana judge John Ferguson, who had rendered the verdict, with violating his constitutional rights as stated in the Fourteenth Amendment.

In 1896, the Supreme Court ruled in *Plessy* v. *Ferguson* that the Fourteenth Amendment applied solely to political equality. Social equality, such as dictating where one sat on a train, could not be regulated by law. If separate but equal accommodations were provided, there was no violation of Plessy's constitutional rights. Justice John Marshall Harlan disagreed with the decision. In his dissent, he said, "Our constitution is color blind and neither knows nor tolerates classes among citizens. . . . [W]e boast of the freedom enjoyed by our people above all other peoples. But it is difficult to reconcile that boast with a state of law which practically puts the brand of servitude and degradation upon a large class of our fellow citizens, our equals before the law. The thin disguise of equal accommodations will not mislead anyone, or atone for the wrong this day done."[1]

Despite the dissenting vote, the decision was final. The Supreme Court had ruled that separate was equal, conferring its blessing on segregation. States passed dozens of segregation laws, making black people virtual outcasts in many parts of the country of their birth. In the South, there were few if any public places where they could use the same facility whites used.

As one of its early goals, the NAACP took on the task of fighting these laws in court and working to get Congress to pass laws to abolish segregation. The or-

A school for freed slaves in Vicksburg, Mississippi

Left: A Klan member
in 1870

Below: The caption for this cartoon, published
a year after the Civil Rights Act of 1875 was
passed, reads: "Of course he wants to vote the
Democratic ticket!" "You're as free as air, ain't
you? Say you are, or I'll blow your black head off!"

Harry Loper's restaurant after the
1908 riot in Springfield, Illinois

The Springfield, Illinois, riot dominated
this page of a Chicago newspaper.

Left: William English Walling, the author of a newspaper article that contributed to the formation of the NAACP

Right: Mary White Ovington, one of the three main founders of the NAACP

Left: Oswald Garrison Villard, publisher of the *New York Evening Post* and grandson of the famous abolitionist William Lloyd Garrison, was another key figure in the founding of the NAACP.

Right: Booker T. Washington was considered to be the primary spokesperson for blacks, but his participation was not solicited by the founders of the NAACP. They felt his views were too conservative.

Left: W.E.B. DuBois, a writer and college professor, would become one of the most important voices of the NAACP.

Right: Joel Spingarn was a charter member of the executive committee of the NAACP.

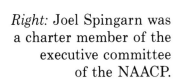

THE CRISIS
A RECORD OF THE DARKER RACES

Volume One   NOVEMBER, 1910   Number One

Edited by W. E. BURGHARDT DU BOIS, with the co-operation of Oswald Garrison Villard,
J. Max Barber, Charles Edward Russell, Kelly Miller, W. S. Braithwaite and M. D. Maclean.

CONTENTS

Along the Color Line   3

Opinion   7

Editorial   10

The N. A. A. C. P.   12

Athens and Browns-
ville   13
By MOORFIELD STOREY

The Burden . . .   14

What to Read . .   15

PUBLISHED MONTHLY BY THE
National Association for the Advancement of Colored People
AT TWENTY VESEY STREET   NEW YORK CITY

ONE ᴅᴏᴸᴸᴀʀ A YEAR   TEN CENTS A COPY

Left: The Crisis was the official magazine of the NAACP. Its first editor was W.E.B. DuBois.

Below: The Spingarn Medal is given annually to honor "the highest and noblest achievement" of a black American. The first medal was given in 1915.

Top: A lynching in the South.
Middle: The NAACP
anti-lynching parade in
1917 in New York City.
Left: In 1919,
James Weldon Johnson
became the NAACP's first
black executive secretary.

An anti-lynching demonstration in June 1922 in Washington, D.C., during the time when an anti-lynch bill was being debated in the U.S. Senate

Dr. L.A. Nixon, whose test case led to a
Supreme Court decision upholding the right
of blacks to vote in a primary election

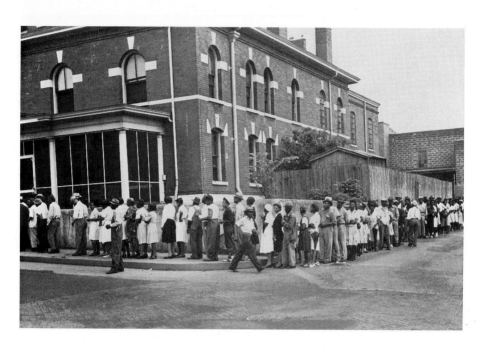

Above: Black voters in Georgia in 1946 turn out despite warnings to stay away from the polls.
Below: Harry Truman (left) addressed the 1947 NAACP annual convention. On the right is Walter White, the NAACP executive secretary. Eleanor Roosevelt is in the middle.

Above: The "colored" entrance to a theater in Florida.
Below: These attorneys successfully argued the
landmark case of *Brown* v. *Topeka Board of
Education*, which said that segregation in
public schools is unconstitutional.
In the middle is Thurgood Marshall.

Federal troops guard black students attending
Little Rock's Central High School in 1957.

Right: Colonel Charles
Young, a black West Point
graduate, was a candidate
to head a division of black
soldiers during World War I.
However, discrimination
by the War Department
kept his ambitions at bay.

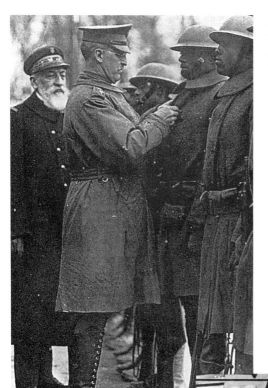

Left: The French awarded many black soldiers the *croix de guerre* during World War I.

Right: Black women contributed to the war effort during World War II.

This volunteer black platoon captured twenty-five
Nazis during World War II.

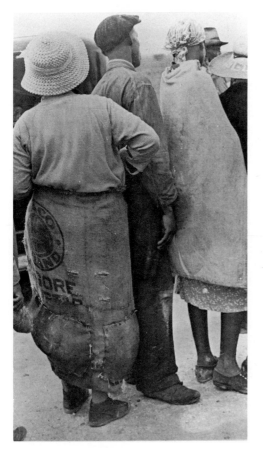

Left: The Great Depression
hit blacks especially hard.

Facing page, top: NAACP
executive director
Roy Wilkins (left) and
Jackson, Mississippi,
branch official Medgar
Evers under arrest as they
attempt to picket a
Woolworth's department
store in Jackson in 1963.
Middle: Benjamin Hooks
executive director of the
NAACP from 1977 to 1992.
Bottom: An award
presentation for the
Act-So program run
by the NAACP to help
black youth do well in
subjects like science,
music, and writing.

An NAACP-sponsored silent march for jobs held in
Washington, D.C., in 1989

ganization focused on two particularly offensive areas of segregation—transportation and housing.

Train and bus stations had separate waiting rooms, ticket windows, and restrooms. Bus companies required blacks to sit in the back of the bus and to give up their seats when the white section filled up. Most trains would not allow blacks in the dining car or provide berths in the sleeping cars. Often the "special" car for blacks was half of the baggage car. This car was usually just behind the engine. Coal dust and fumes drifted in from the engine area. When there was a train wreck, the first car was usually badly damaged, and blacks often suffered severe injuries. To add to the misery of the black traveler, white men often came to the black car to smoke and drink. Smoking and drinking was not allowed in the white cars.

In 1915, the NAACP prepared a petition to the Interstate Commerce Commission (ICC), the federal agency that regulated transportation. The petition included carefully collected documentation and photographs of segregation in the South on trains, in station waiting rooms, and in dining areas. But the entry of the country into World War I and the government's preoccupation with the war effort prevented the presentation of the petition to the ICC.

In 1917, the NAACP mounted other efforts to fight segregated transportation. Lawyers began preparing a case protesting discrimination by the Atcheson, Topeka, and Santa Fe Railway against W. Scott Brown, a black Oklahoma NAACP official. The intention was to bring the case to the Supreme Court, should the decision be unfavorable in the lower court. Here again, the attention to the war intervened and made it impossible to bring the Brown case before the Supreme Court.

Then the NAACP turned from its legal tactic to publicity, striving to get others to pressure the ICC. A letter of protest was sent to President Woodrow Wilson. Copies went to northern and southern newspaper editors. During the years after the war, the NAACP continued without success to press the ICC to take some action.

The NAACP turned to the courts in a new legal strategy to get the transportation segregation laws overturned. Supporting blacks who defied the laws, the organization began to see some success.

In 1918, the Baltimore NAACP branch won two victories against the Washington, Baltimore, and Indiana line, in Maryland courts, overturning an indictment against a black man who had refused to sit in a segregated car and winning a segregation suit for a black woman doctor. Thereafter, that railroad line took no action against black people who defied its segregation policies.

In 1941, with the support of the NAACP, Illinois congressman Arthur Mitchell, who had been thrown off a Pullman car in Arkansas because he was black, won a discrimination suit in the Supreme Court. The court ruled that denial of sleeping and dining accommodations on trains was unconstitutional. Implementing this ruling meant extra expense for railroads following the separate-but-equal rule because they had to haul extra dining and Pullman cars. The railroads provided separate dining areas by using a curtain to separate white and black diners.

In 1944, Irene Morgan defied a bus driver's order to move to the back of a Greyhound bus traveling through Virginia to Maryland. She was jailed for violating Virginia's segregation laws. The NAACP took her case through the court process to the Supreme Court, which ruled that being required to provide separate seating was an undue burden on bus companies providing transportation from state to state. The ruling meant that buses crossing state lines could not be segregated.

In 1950, in *Henderson* v. *United States,* Alpha Phi Alpha, a black fraternity, won a Supreme Court ruling that racial segregation in dining cars was unconstitutional. The NAACP supported the case as a friend of the court.

By the early 1950s, many of the humiliating vestiges of segregated interstate travel were gone.

While segregated transportation restricted blacks' freedom to travel, perhaps the most painful aspect of segregation for black people has been its effects on finding a place to live. *Plessy* v. *Ferguson* doctrine encouraged communities to pass laws requiring blacks to live only in certain parts of town. Not only was segregated housing one more degrading aspect of life for blacks, but the limitations on places where blacks could live produced severe housing shortages. In most cities, many blacks were forced to cram their families into already crowded areas.

Some white real estate speculators were quick to see an opportunity for profit in this unfortunate situation. They bought large houses and subdivided them into small apartments that they then rented to blacks. Desperate for a place to live, blacks paid the high rents that were charged. Then the owners requested a lowering of real estate taxes from the city because the presence of blacks lowered property values. As more and more blacks crowded into the buildings, wear and tear took its toll. Landlords spent little on upkeep and repair. Black tenants with no place else to go didn't complain because they feared eviction. The city didn't care and seldom enforced its zoning and health regulations. A slum was created. With such an arrangement—high rents, low upkeep, and low taxes—a landlord could get rich, and many did.[2]

Within those slum walls in many a well-scrubbed

but shabby room grew the yearning for pleasant, airy rooms—a decent place to live, like those seen in magazines and movies. It was for these basic yearnings, actually the right of black people to live in places of their choice, that the NAACP waged a battle against segregation in housing.

The first housing segregation law was passed by the city of Baltimore in 1910. Dozens of other cities in the South followed Baltimore's lead—Winston-Salem, Richmond, Dallas, Atlanta, New Orleans, and Louisville.

In 1914, a controversy between a white man and a black man brought on by the Louisville segregation law drew the support of the NAACP. This was a case the NAACP believed it could win in the Supreme Court. A white man sued a black man because the black man had refused to honor an agreement to buy a house, claiming that it was on a block where he was not permitted to live because of the segregation ordinance. A Kentucky court ruled that the ordinance was valid. The NAACP appealed the verdict to the Supreme Court, which overturned the ordinance in November 1917. The high court said the ordinance "destroyed the right of the individual to acquire, enjoy, and dispose of his property" and was a violation of the Fourteenth Amendment.

The ruling was clear: Segregated housing laws were unconstitutional. But two cities, New Orleans and Richmond, wouldn't give up. They thought that a change in the wording of their regulations might make them valid. The NAACP took the cities to the Supreme Court, which ruled their reworded ordinances unconstitutional.

Many black people tested their right to buy houses in white neighborhoods. Some suffered at the hands of white mobs. In 1919, twenty-three blacks and fifteen whites were killed in a riot started by a white homeowners' organization that opposed blacks' moving into their Chicago neighborhood. In 1924, Garfield Heights, Ohio, whites forced a number of black homeowners out of their homes. In 1926 in Denver, whites tore down a house recently purchased by a black.

Meanwhile in 1917, segregationist property owners devised a new tactic. They wrote restrictive covenants into their deed abstracts. Such covenants had been used on the West Coast to keep Asians from living in certain areas.

A typical restrictive covenant is the following one, taken from the deed abstract for a plot of land in Columbus, Ohio. It is dated November 1, 1924.

> The occupancy by a colored family of a single residence on said street would destroy immediately a large percentage of the value of said property, would make it difficult to rent or sell the same and would result in a decrease of the rental if the same is rented and decrease of the purchase price if the same is sold. . . . Each of said owners hereby agree and binds himself, his heirs, executors, and administrators never to sell, lease, mortgage, pledge, give or otherwise dispose of in any way the property above mentioned to any colored person or persons, never to rent said premises to any colored person or persons or permit any colored person to use or occupy the premises owned by him except as a servant working for the white family. . . . By the term colored persons is meant any person in whole or in part of the Negro race or blood and any person other than a member of the white or Caucasian race. . . . Any contract shall be void if the purchaser be a colored person.

Restrictive covenants, which often applied to Jews and other minorities as well as to blacks, called for penalties if they were violated. They were made valid for ninety-nine years, far beyond the lifetime of the first owner. The property could not, in the foreseeable future, be sold to a black person.

In 1917, the NAACP began a thirty-year battle to end restrictive covenants. In 1926, the Supreme Court rendered a decision in an NAACP case, upholding restrictive covenants, and for twenty years thereafter the high court refused to hear any cases on restrictive covenants. Finally, in 1948, it reviewed five cases brought by the NAACP. In a 6-to-1 decision, the high court declared that the Fourteenth Amendment protected the property rights of black people, noting that property rights were a basic civil right and that restrictive covenants could not be enforced. The ruling did not stop racists from writing the restrictive covenants.

In 1949, the NAACP began to focus its attention on the segregation policies of federal agencies such as the Federal Housing Authority (FHA), established in 1933 to help low-income families purchase homes. The FHA policy encouraged housing segregation, calling for a racially restrictive covenant to protect against "inharmonious racial groups."[3] Other government agencies, such as the Federal Home Loan Bank Board and the Homeowners Loan Corporation, also encouraged segregated housing.

In February 1949, the NAACP submitted a twenty-one-page report to President Harry Truman, charging the FHA with supporting and perpetuating housing segregation. The attorney general responded in December with the announcement that the government would end policies that contributed to the creation of racial ghettos.[4] But it didn't happen.

In 1953, a California court ruled that the government's housing segregation policy was a violation of the Fourteenth Amendment. Government lawyers appealed the decision to the Supreme Court. The high court, referring to its previous decisions in the NAACP 1917 segregation law case and the 1948 restrictive covenant case, refused to hear the case. By the 1960s, however, the government still had not changed its policy.

In August 1961, NAACP executive director Roy Wilkins, as chairman of the lobbying organization the Leadership Conference on Civil Rights, presented a sixty-page report titled "Federally Supported Discrimination" to President John F. Kennedy. The report described federally supported racial discrimination and called upon the president to create a civil rights code "governing the executive branch of the government" and to direct all departments and agencies of the federal government to assure nondiscrimination in all of its activities, programs, institutions and services.[5]

Nearly a year later, in November 1962, President Kennedy responded with Executive Order 11063 on equal opportunity in housing. The order directed "all government agencies and departments in the executive branch of the federal government insofar as their functions relate to the provision, rehabilitation, or operation of housing and related facilities to take all action necessary and appropriate to prevent discrimination because of race, color, creed, or national origin."[6] The order would be enforced through federal funding. Those builders, local agencies, and local public housing authorities who practiced segregation would lose their federal funding.

While the government was changing its housing policy, across the land, many banks were not lending home mortgage money to blacks, and real estate agents were not showing houses in certain areas to blacks. NAACP lobbyist Clarence Mitchell began to work for a law that would, once and for all, desegregate housing. Through meetings with many senators and congresspersons, he formed a strong group of Congressional supporters who wrote and sponsored a housing bill. In 1968, Congress passed the Fair Housing Act, which provided "for fair housing throughout the United States."

By the 1970s, many blacks started to realize their dream of fair and open housing. Problems still existed, and continue to exist, with discrimination by realtors, intolerance of neighbors, and restrictive policies of some banks. But any official or unofficial institutionalization of restrictions is no longer supported by state and federal laws.

VII

FIGHTING THE CASTE OF COLOR IN EDUCATION

While the NAACP viewed segregation on trains and buses and in housing as a serious assault on the rights of blacks, it saw segregation and discrimination in education as a fundamental denial of black citizenship. The uneducated black was unable to make good use of the other rights of an American citizen. Further, an uneducated black population was a drag on the progress of the nation as a whole because uneducated people sometimes need a wide range of social services to survive.

Realizing that the core of the problem was lack of state resources, the NAACP began a campaign to secure federal aid for education for all schools. In 1916, an NAACP education committee issued a call for federal aid to state governments to provide vocational and agricultural education, upgrade rural schools, eliminate illiteracy, and establish education programs for immigrants. In 1917, Congress did pass the Smith-Hughes bill, which provided for federal support of vocational training and for teacher training in agriculture, industrial arts, and home economics. But during the early part of the twentieth century, the NAACP struggled in vain to get legislation that would equalize educational opportunities for blacks.

During these years, as some blacks migrated North, some northern schools began segregating black and white children. In 1915, the Hartford, Connecticut, NAACP chapter was founded to fight segregation in the city schools. The branch set up special classes for black children to counter the assertion by Hartford teachers that black children were ill-prepared to attend the city schools. The NAACP branch was successful in eliminating school segregation in Hartford.

NAACP branches also fought school segregation in other northern states such as Indiana, Pennsylvania, Ohio, and Michigan, with mixed success. In 1917, the Ypsilanti, Michigan, branch did manage to get a court injunction that closed a segregated school. In 1919, Kansas branches joined in defeating a state law calling for separate schools for black children in smaller towns.

That same year, a young Harvard student, Charles Garland, inherited $1 million from his father. He used most of the money to establish the American Fund for Public Service. During the 1920s, the NAACP was the recipient of a number of grants from the fund. One large grant was earmarked to fund a well-based civil rights campaign. In 1930, the NAACP used some of the funds to commission a study of the status of the civil rights of black people. The study was done by Nathan R. Margold, a former assistant U.S. attorney for the Southern District of New York. He surveyed all known court decisions, public budgets, and records on unequal allotment of funds to schools, discrimination by property holders, denial of the vote to blacks, lynchings, job discrimination, segregated travel, and other civil rights issues.

Looking back, Margold found a picture of education for blacks in the South after *Plessy* v. *Ferguson* that was certainly separate but just as certainly not equal. In the South in 1916, schools spent $10.30 per year to educate each white student and $2.89 to educate each black student. The school "year" for blacks lasted three to four months, compared with six to nine months for whites. Many blacks had to attend classes in churches, stores, and private homes. Black parents hoping to improve education for their children held fundraisers to pay for a few more months of school and to help pay teachers. Many cities provided no high school or college education to blacks. There were a few small trade colleges for blacks, but southern blacks had no opportunity to study professions such as law or medicine in the South.

While the study of education formed a large part of this report, Margold also reported on many other phases of the lives of blacks in America. The Margold report provided a portrayal of an immense problem and caused the NAACP to change its tactics, shifting from defending those blacks with grievances to mounting a frontal attack on segregation itself.

Charles Houston, a black lawyer and Howard Law School vice-dean who had achieved a brilliant academic record at Amherst College and Harvard Law School, was hired as the NAACP's first lawyer in 1935. In 1936, Thurgood Marshall, one of Houston's top students at Howard University, signed on as Houston's assistant. Houston saw education as key to blacks' achieving full rights as American citizens: "Discrimination in education is symbolic of all the more drastic discriminations. . . . Economically inferior education makes negroes less able to stand competition with whites for jobs," he said, noting that a poor education makes it difficult for "young Negro men and women to be courageous and aggressive in defense of their rights."[1]

As he surveyed the Margold information, Houston determined that of all black students, those barred from admission to state professional schools had the greatest need for immediate help. For them, there was no education, separate or not. Separate but equal was the law. He decided that his tactic would be to press for separate but equal professional schools. The states would come to see that since a separate-but-equal law school or medical school was too expensive, the states would have to admit black students to existing schools—and segregation would end.

In a series of legal cases overseen by Houston, the NAACP fought for the right of blacks to enter southern professional schools.

– In 1935, Donald Murray applied to the University of Maryland law school and was turned down despite a good academic record at Amherst College (Massachusetts), an integrated private school. The NAACP took the University of Maryland to court, claiming that as a citizen with rights guaranteed by the Fourteenth Amendment, Murray had the right to be admitted to the state law school. The case received a great deal of publicity. As the testimony and debate focused on providing a separate-but-equal law school for blacks, public opinion opposing the extra expense grew. The local Baltimore court refused admission to Murray, but the Maryland court of appeals ordered his admission. Murray entered the Maryland law school and graduated with honors four years later.

– Honor student Lloyd Gaines applied unsuccessfully to the University of Missouri law school after working his way through Lincoln University, a black college. The NAACP took his case through the Missouri courts to the Supreme Court, which ruled in 1938 that the university had to admit Gaines or provide equal facilities within the state. A few years later, the state established a law school in an old building that once housed a hair dressing school. Gaines, who had since enrolled in the University of Michigan, refused to attend the school. While the NAACP was preparing a case to require Missouri to defend the equality of the new law school for blacks, Gaines disappeared. But the Gaines case still raised the question of whether a professional school set up for blacks could be equal to an existing school from which they were excluded.

– The same question again came up when Ada Lois Sipuel applied and was refused admission to the University of Oklahoma law school. Sipuel appealed to the NAACP for help, and NAACP lawyers took her case to the Supreme Court. The high court ordered the state of Oklahoma to provide legal education to her "as soon as it does for applicants of any other group." Oklahoma proceeded to set up a law school in the state capitol building in twelve days. Its opening coincided with the University of Oklahoma's class registration date. Sipuel refused to attend the school, which attracted just one student and closed after eighteen months. A court found the black law school to be unequal to the University of Oklahoma law school and ordered the University of Oklahoma to admit Sipuel.

– The success of the Sipuel case caused a number of blacks to apply for admission to various graduate programs in universities in the South. Some southern universities set up segregated sections in classes. The NAACP fought this tactic, and universities were eventually forced to desegregate. In one 1950 case, George McLaurin, who was pursuing his Ph.D. at the University of Oklahoma, was forced to sit in a segregated alcove off a classroom. The NAACP took this case to the Supreme Court. The court ruled that McLaurin be admitted to the College of Education and be treated like other students because segregated treatment would "interfere with his ability to study, to engage in discussion and exchange views with other students and in general to learn his profession.[2]

– When Heman Sweatt sought admission to the University of Texas law school in 1950, the Texas courts gave the state six months to set up a separate law school. The NAACP took the case to the Supreme Court, which in a 1950 decision ruled that a school set up in six months in three rented rooms was not the educational equal of the University of Texas law school.

The Sweatt and McLaurin decisions brought the Supreme Court perilously close to overturning the *Plessy v. Ferguson* separate-but-equal doctrine. The stage was set for the NAACP's next move.

Thurgood Marshall, who had succeeded Charles Houston as chief NAACP counsel, read those two decisions very carefully. He found, as he wrote to a fellow lawyer, "road markings telling us where to go."[3] He could see that it was time to abandon fighting for separate-but-equal education for blacks and to focus on abolishing segregated education. Since the 1930s, the NAACP had waged campaigns in the courts for better school buildings, buses, longer school terms, and equal funds for white and black education. In the South, black teachers had historically been paid much less than white teachers in the same school system. Between 1936 and 1950, fifty court battles for equalization of teacher salaries were fought in thirteen states, winning $3 million in additional salaries for black teachers.

Now, in 1950, it was time to get segregated education abolished and to fight in the name of the millions of black elementary and high school students who were getting a segregated education. This time the argument would be that segregation harms black children because it makes them feel inferior. Experts on education and psychology would be brought into the court to testify.

Even as Marshall studied the cases and consulted his experts, a brave band of black parents in South Carolina decided to act. Clarendon County was a place where everyone—white and black—was poor. There, the lyncher and the Ku Klux Klan terrorized blacks at will. When several petitions to the county school board for better schools for black children met with no results, parents appealed to the NAACP for help. It was just the kind of case that Marshall was seeking— the opportunity he needed to bring the issue of school segregation to the attention of the Supreme Court. In May 1950, the NAACP sued the Clarendon County school board in South Carolina federal district court, requesting that the board "be restrained from making a distinction on account of race and color in maintaining public schools for Negro children which are inferior to those maintained for white children."[4] In a pretrial hearing, the NAACP announced its intention to end segregation through the suit. The court ruling upheld segregation and ordered the school board to furnish equal educational opportunities to black children. But Marshall continued to pursue abolishing segregation and filed such a plea for the Clarendon County parents with the Supreme Court.

During the court sessions, the parents who had begun the effort for their children were feeling the effects of the worst that the racists of Clarendon County had to offer. Banks called mortgages on homes and farms. Homes went up in flames in the middle of the night. Black neighborhoods were terrorized by people firing shotguns from speeding cars. One minister was run out of town. But through it all, the parents stood fast.

In other parts of the country, other black parents were mounting similar efforts. In Prince Edward County, Virginia; Wilmington, Delaware; and Washington, D.C., parents, with the assistance of the NAACP, filed similar suits in federal district courts. In one 1950 case, the parents of eight-year-old Linda Brown sued the Board of Education in Topeka, Kansas, because it refused to admit their daughter to her neighborhood school. The federal district court in Kansas, while agreeing that "segregation of white and colored children in the public schools has a detrimental effect upon colored children," ruled that segregation was constitutional.

The Supreme Court heard all five cases as one case under the heading *Brown* v. *Board of Education of Topeka, Kansas* on December 8 and 9, 1952, but failed to come to a decision. New hearings were scheduled for December 1953. The court requested that Marshall and the other attorneys arguing the cases be prepared to debate the intent of Congress and the states when they approved the Fourteenth Amendment. Did the amendment ban racial segregation? Did Congress or the courts have the authority to abolish racial segregation? How and when should segregation be ended? For five months after the second hearing, the NAACP awaited the court's verdict.

The NAACP would come to call May 17, 1954, Decision Monday—the day the Supreme Court handed down its decision on school segregation in *Brown* v. *Board of Education*. In part, the decision read:

We cannot turn back the clock to 1868 when Plessy v Ferguson was written. We must consider public education in light of its full development and its present place in American life throughout the nation. Only in this way can it be determined if segregation in public schools deprives these plaintiffs of the equal protection of the laws—it is doubtful that any child may be reasonably expected to succeed in life if he is denied the opportunity of an education. Such an opportunity, where the state has undertaken to provide it, is a right which must be made available to all on equal terms.... We come then to the question presented: Does segregation of children in public schools solely on the basis of race, even though the physical factor and other tangible factors may be equal, deprive the children of the minority group of equal educational opportunities? We believe it does. To separate them from others of similar age and qualifications, solely because of their race generates a feeling of inferiority as to their status in the community that may affect their hearts and minds in a way unlikely to ever be undone.... We conclude that in the field of public education the doctrine of separate-but-equal has no place. Separate educational facilities are inherently unequal.[5]

The verdict was in. The highest court in the land had called for an end to school segregation and, by condemning the separate-but-equal doctrine of *Plessy* v. *Ferguson,* had issued its view of all segregation.

Jubilantly, *The Crisis* saluted the decision: "The United States Supreme Court handed down a historic decision on May 17. By declaring racial segregation in the public schools to be unconstitutional, the court took a step which will inevitably destroy present forms of segregation wherever practiced. The separate-but-equal fiction, as legal doctrine, now joins the horsecar, the bustle, and the five-cent cigar."[6]

The NAACP went to work to facilitate the implementation of the decision. All branches were instructed to petition their local school boards to abolish segregation without delay. Thurgood Marshall called a meeting of seventeen NAACP branch officials in Atlanta, Georgia. They discussed assisting school boards in working out ways and means of desegregating schools. They issued the Atlanta Declaration, which pledged all their resources "to work with other law-abiding citizens who are anxious to translate this decision into a program of action to eradicate racial segregation in public education as speedily as possible."[7]

The battle would be a long one for the NAACP. Newspaper clippings gave a clue of the die-hard segregationist attitudes toward the Supreme Court decision. "It means racial strife of the bitterest sort. Mississippi cannot and will not try to abide by such a decision," read an editorial in the Jackson (Mississippi) *Daily News*.[8] The *Huntsville* (Alabama) *Times* called the decision "a great shock . . . a crushing blow to all the customs, traditions, and modes, extending over more than 200 years, that have been built up or grown up around the principle and practice of segregation."[9]

Reconvening in October 1955 to decide on the implementation of its decision, the Supreme Court decided not to set a deadline for implementation. Instead, it directed that a prompt and reasonable start be made to abolish school segregation "with all deliberate speed."[10]

Even before the implementation order had been issued, the District of Columbia and some states, including Maryland, Delaware, New Mexico, Missouri, West Virginia, Arkansas, and Oklahoma, were earnestly going about the business of desegregating their schools. In other states, public officials such as South Carolina governor James Byrnes led the way in declaring, "Never!" The White Citizens Council, dedicated to maintaining second-class citizenship for blacks, formed chapters in many of Mississippi's eighty-two counties. Similar organizations, such as the National Association for the Advancement of White People and the National Association for the Advancement and Protection of White People, were formed. Some whites began plans to start their own private schools and thus keep their children separate from black children. When public schools opened in Fall 1954, Alabama, Georgia, Louisiana, Mississippi, North Carolina, South Carolina, Tennessee, Texas, and Virginia had done nothing to desegregate and had no plans to do so.

In 1957 in Little Rock, Arkansas, Governor Orval Faubus called out the National Guard to keep a group of nine black teenagers from enrolling in Little Rock's Central High in an NAACP-sponsored effort. The NAACP pressured President Dwight Eisenhower to take direct action to desegregate the school but had no success. Finally, Faubus complied with a court order and pulled out the Guard from the school. Angry mobs surrounded the school and threatened the students. Eisenhower federalized the Guard and sent in paratroopers to protect the students as they entered and left the school. The battle was not over for the students. They endured harassment and racial slurs at the hands of a small group of students for most of the rest of the school year. The nine students and the NAACP Little Rock branch president, Daisy Bates, shared the NAACP's Spingarn Medal in 1958.

Because many southern school systems were defying the Supreme Court order, it began to appear that a Supreme Court case would be needed to accomplish desegregation in each of the die-hard states, perhaps even in many communities in these states. For nine years that was the case. Finally, in a 1969 case, the Supreme Court, weary of dealing with evasions of *Brown*

v. *Board of Education* ruled that "all deliberate speed" was no longer operative. The court ruled that all segregated schools must be abolished immediately.

Through the 1970s, desegregation of the schools continued. By 1980, the NAACP could report that a smaller percentage of blacks attended mostly black schools in the South than in any other part of the country. The problems were actually in the North, where white flight to the suburbs had left major cities like Detroit to the blacks, leaving the urban schools virtually segregated. The NAACP and other groups then began the bitter battle over busing students across city and suburban boundaries and addressing the urban problems that had produced segregated inner-city areas.

But nearly gone were the days of separate-but-equal. Decision Monday had begun the process that changed the world for black Americans.

VIII

**TO SERVE THE NATION
AS FREE AMERICANS**

Perhaps most disheartening to black people has been
the discrimination and segregation endured at the
hands of their own government. Certainly it was ironic
that even black employees of the "land of the free and
the home of the brave" did not enjoy their full rights as
Americans.

In 1913, the wife of the newly elected president,
Mrs. Woodrow Wilson, visited several government department offices. There, the Georgia-born first lady
found something that surprised her. Black clerks and
white clerks were working in the same office. They
shared the same lunch room. Shortly after her visit,
new rules of segregation were announced for the Bureau of Census, the Bureau of Printing and Engraving,
the Treasury Department, and the Post Office Department. Signs went up, directing that blacks could not
eat in the dining room. Instead, they had to eat in the
toilet areas. Black men and white women could not
share office areas. Separate toilet areas were set up for
blacks and whites.

NAACP officials—chairman Oswald Villard in particular—felt betrayed. They had supported Wilson's election, urging blacks to vote for a candidate who had promised that "Negroes can count on me for absolute fair dealing and for help in advancing the interests of their race in the United States."[1]

Villard sent a written protest to President Wilson, pointing out that black voters helped put him in office because they believed he would support their rights as Americans. Wilson replied that segregation in government offices would relieve the friction between blacks and whites and "by putting certain bureaus and sections of the service in charge of Negroes we are rendering them more safe in their possession of office and less likely to be discriminated against."[2]

Shortly thereafter, six black men were dismissed from the Internal Revenue Service after thirteen years of service. They were replaced with white men. Dismissals of blacks in the Post Office Department followed. Discrimination spread to the Capitol building, the Library of Congress, and other government offices. Blacks applying for government jobs were told there had been a mistake; there were no openings.

Segregation and discrimination by the federal government set an example that the nation followed. Discrimination and racial violence increased throughout the country. W. E. B. DuBois would write in *The Crisis* that Wilson "is one of the most greivous disappointments, a disappointed people must bear."[3]

In the armed services, blacks were segregated and given menial assignments in kitchens and hospitals. In 1917, shortly after the United States entered World War I, the NAACP called an Afro-American conference in Washington to discuss issues related to the war and black people. The conference called on blacks to join the war effort despite the racial injustices in the country. The NAACP was determined to make certain that blacks participating in the war effort were treated fairly. The conference called for the right of blacks to serve in battle and not just in kitchens and warehouses and to be officers and to receive officer training.

Board member Joel Spingarn was certain the army and President Wilson would not allow whites and blacks to train together. Shortly before war was declared, working on his own and without NAACP support, Spingarn had proposed the idea of a separate camp for training black army officers who could lead black troops. The army agreed to set up such a camp if Spingarn could recruit two hundred men. Spingarn found two hundred volunteers by putting out an open letter calling for "educated colored men." The army raised the number to 250. Spingarn went to Howard University, a black university in Washington, D.C., looking for more recruits. As an incentive, he offered to buy their uniforms, which would be a major expense for the men. By the time war was declared in April, he had 350 black volunteers for officer training. Most were college students or graduates.

Spingarn's idea received a lot of criticism from blacks, including NAACP officials. It was called "the rankest kind of segregation" and "a tacit approval of segregation" by two board members.[4] One black newspaper commented that "Negroes had no business segregating themselves until the government had made it clear that it intended to segregate them."[5] Spingarn defended the segregated camp idea in speeches and newspaper interviews. He said that the segregated camp was temporary, forced on blacks by circumstances, but that it could change their role in the war, providing the chance to become leaders and officers rather than privates.

At this point, Spingarn was called off to the army himself, leaving the NAACP to wrestle with the issue. Finally, after a great deal of debate, the NAACP board adopted a resolution supporting the camp. The resolution read, "Rather than have no officers' training camp for colored men, who under the new draft law are to be placed in separate regiments, this Association favors separate training camps for colored officers."[6] When the Department of War announced that the camps would open June 17, 1917, in Des Moines, Iowa, *The Crisis* triumphantly informed its readers, "We have won. The camp is granted; we shall have 1,000 Negro officers in the United States Army. Write to us for information."[7] From this point on, the NAACP proceeded to take credit for the camp, although Spingarn had proposed it, recruited the men, and dealt with the army on his own without NAACP support or direction.

The first class of 630 black officers graduated on October 17, 1917. Colonel Charles Young, a black West Point graduate, seemed a natural to head a black army division. Mary Ovington, an NAACP staff member, wrote, "I saw young East side boys in their new uniforms, gathered around him drinking in every word he said. Could he have been placed at the head of Negro soldiers, led by the new Negro officers, the success of his Division would have been assured."

But the army would have no black generals. It retired Colonel Young early on the grounds that he was disabled because he had high blood pressure. The NAACP investigated and found Colonel Young's health to be good, making it obvious that the army did not want to promote a black man to general.

Reinstatement of Colonel Young, as well as a number of other demands, was on an NAACP list delivered to Secretary of War Newton Baker by W. E. B. DuBois. While accepting the reality that the army would be segregated into all-white and all-black divisions, the NAACP demanded more responsibility for blacks and for the admission of blacks to the navy, air corps, and army artillery.

The War Department temporarily reinstated Colonel Young to stateside command in Rockford, Illinois, but most of the other NAACP demands were met with disdain. In fact, the War Department reported that only a limited number of black physicians would be accepted as medical officers, just enough to serve black troops. The others probably would serve as privates. No blacks would be allowed to serve in the nurse corps.

The NAACP uncovered many abuses of black soldiers. They were often forced to work under unhealthy conditions and threatened with long terms in the stockade if they objected. White soldiers would not salute black officers. Blacks in training often fell prey to the bigoted local customs in the towns near their camps. In Kansas, black soldiers from Camp Funston were forced to sit in the balcony of a theater. C. C. Ballou, the white general commanding the camp, issued a directive that supported the right of the black troops to sit where they pleased but directed them to follow the local custom for the good of the service.

The NAACP demanded fair treatment of black recruits and worked to protect the rights of black soldiers in training camps. The Boston branch sent a protest to the War Department about personal abuse by officers, such as calling black soldiers "nigger" and "coon" and assaulting them. The War Department issued a general order banning abusive language.

There were frequent cases of police brutality against black troops by military and civilian police. In August 1917, a batallion of black soldiers, their nerves made raw by Houston police brutality, started a riot. Seventeen whites and two blacks were killed. A total of 124 black soldiers were court-martialed; 13 were found guilty and hanged, 16 were sentenced to death, and the rest given prison terms.

The NAACP investigated the case and found that the soldiers had sought to avenge the brutal beating of a popular corporal. The corporal had been attacked by police when he went to the defense of a black woman being mistreated by Houston policemen. An NAACP delegation petitioned President Wilson, who commuted the death sentences of ten of the men and affirmed six of the death sentences. The six men were quickly hanged. The rest of the men remained in prison. The NAACP continued to press the case of the "Houston Martyrs," and in 1938, President Franklin Roosevelt finally ordered the release of the last prisoner.

The NAACP also worked to support blacks in combat. As black soldiers went off to serve in the battle zone in France, reports came back that black officers were cowards and black troops were rapists. When the war ended, the NAACP sent *Crisis* editor DuBois to France. His mission was to investigate these reports, write up his findings, and publish them in *The Crisis*—in other words to discover and write the true story of the black soldier in France.

DuBois found the same discrimination and segregation in foreign service that blacks endured in their own land. Black officers who had so triumphantly graduated in Des Moines had been systematically replaced with white officers.[9] The charge was inefficiency. But in fact, the black officer had often been denied the special training he needed and then been called "unfit for the job."[10] Some black officers were trained by the French. Certainly the French army hadn't found black officers unfit since the French Gondricourt Training School had praised its black officer trainees.[11]

In some cases, no reason had been given for dismissing a black officer. One black intelligence and personnel officer had been dismissed and reinstated three times because the white officers assigned to his duties could not do the work.

General Ballou, who commanded the all-black 92nd Division, had often referred to his troops as the "rapist division." But DuBois found that only one soldier of the 92nd had been convicted of rape and two of intent to rape. "It is doubtful if another division of the U.S. Army had a better record," wrote DuBois. DuBois also wrote to twenty-one mayors of French towns where the black troops were billeted and asked them how black troops conducted themselves. Back came replies such as, "They have earned our high regard by their discipline and their faultless behavior." "Won the esteem and sympathy of all the population." "Good conduct, good discipline, fine spirit."[12]

DuBois uncovered one army document that urged French people to discriminate against black soldiers, and he published it in *The Crisis*. The opportunity to read such a document provided both blacks and whites with an insight into how discrimination was justified by bigots. It was a chilling document.

The document was entitled "Secret Information Concerning Black Troops." It began:

It is important for French officers who have been called upon to exercise command over black American troops, or to live in close contact with them to have an exact idea of the position occupied by Negroes in the United States.... American opinion is unanimous on the color question and does not admit of any discussion.... The increasing number of Negroes in the United States would create for the white race in the Republic a menace of degeneracy were it not that an impassable gulf has been made between them.... Although a citizen of the United States, the black man is regarded as an inferior being, with whom relations of business or service only are possible. The black is constantly being censured for his want of intelligence and discretion, his lack of civic and professional conscience and for his tendency toward undue familiarity. The vices of the Negro are a constant menace to the American who has to repress them sternly. For instance, the black American troops in France have, by themselves, given rise to as many complaints for attempted rape as all the rest of the army.[13]

When the French ministry heard of the document, it confiscated all of the copies it could find and burned them. The propaganda had little effect on French townspeople. At first some were afraid, but most welcomed black troops into their homes and listened to the sad tales of racial injustice in the United States.

Despite the racial indignities, black troops did their part to win the war. Engineer and labor batallions built roads, bridges, and railroads; salvaged equipment from battlefields; and restored French farmland torn apart by battle trenches. Black troops such as the 370th regiment of the 93rd Division, which fought at St. Mihiel in France, captured several sectors and won sixteen American Distinguished Service Crosses and seventy-five French Croix de Guerre.[14] Proudly, DuBois reported this to *Crisis* readers. Blacks read about the contributions of their troops and knew they were not rapists or cowards but heroes.

Black soldiers resisted the taunts of German propaganda which asked, "Do you enjoy the same rights as the white people do in America, the land of freedom and democracy, or are you rather treated over there as second-class citizens? . . . Throw away your guns, come over to the German lines. You will find friends who will help you."[15]

When the armistice was signed in November 1918, black servicemen returned home determined more than ever to win their rights in the country they had fought for. But at home they found whites who resented the status blacks had attained in the service and whites who feared blacks trained in combat. By the summer of 1919, those white fears were the main ingredient in setting off Red Summer, when twenty-six cities across the country erupted into race riots.

More than twenty years later, the United States found itself on the verge of entering another war—World War II. On September 14, 1940, President Roosevelt signed the Selective Service Act, which would draft the men needed to build up the U.S. Army. Still, the army was segregated. The navy assigned all blacks to work as waiters and cooks. The air corps and the marines did not admit blacks. Once more, it appeared that segregation and discrimination would be a part of the lives of black servicemen going off to defend democracy.

The NAACP renewed its effort to win a fair chance for black servicepeople. Walter White, NAACP executive secretary; A. Philip Randolph, head of the Brotherhood of Sleeping Car Porters; and Arnold Hill, head of the Urban League, met with President Roosevelt. The civil rights leaders presented the president with a list of demands. Black officers, including nurses and doctors, should be integrated into all army units. Black reserve officers should be assigned as instructors. Black soldiers should receive the same training as white soldiers. Blacks should be appointed to draft boards. Black civilian aides should be appointed to the staff of the secretaries of the navy and army.

The President promised to do what he could to reduce discrimination and integrate the armed forces. The black leaders left with high hopes, but it was nearly two weeks before an announcement came from the White House, and when it came, it was stunningly disappointing. Steven Early, White House press secretary, issued a news release that said segregation in the army would continue and that with the exception of the three existing black regiments, all new black units would be commanded by white officers. Early had added on his own that White, Randolph, and Hill had endorsed the new policy.

A storm of angry questions broke over the offices of the three black leaders. They issued a statement that included a copy of the list of demands they had given to the president. "Official approval by the Commander-In-Chief of the army and navy of such discrimination and segregation is a stab in the back of democracy," the statement read in part.[16]

While the president did not back down on segregation, he did issue an order that "Negro organizations will be established in each major branch of the service."[17] Roosevelt also appointed black civilian aides to two key defense agencies: Judge William Hastie as civilian aide to the secretary of war and Colonel Campbell Johnson assistant to the director of Selective Service. The idea was that these two men would be in a position to promote the interests of blacks in these agencies.

The NAACP also focused its attention on discrimination in factories that made weapons, vehicles, and supplies for the war. The only job openings for blacks in these plants were low-paying jobs such as janitors and kitchen workers. The NAACP appealed to the president and to other Washington officials to use their power as the ones who controlled government defense contracts to stop this discrimination.

The NAACP sent copies of new defense contracts to the 1,200 NAACP branches, urging branch members to circulate the information to qualified black workers so that they could apply for the jobs required to fill the contract. Records of all refusals were to be sent to the national NAACP office. As more and more defense contracts were written, the list of those blacks refused jobs grew. The NAACP presented this record to Washington officials to prove that qualified blacks were not being hired.

Walter White wrote an article entitled "It's Our Country Too" for *The Saturday Evening Post*. The article gave the facts about discrimination in the defense factories and was called a revelation by many readers. At the time the *Post* article was published, newspapers were reporting a shortage of defense workers.

At the urging of the NAACP, four senators sponsored a resolution to initiate a Senate investigation of discrimination in defense plants, but the resolution never emerged from the Senate committee studying it.

Despite sustained pressure by the NAACP, the government did nothing. Black Americans became increasingly bitter over the situation. A. Philip Randolph, head of the Brotherhood of Sleeping Car Porters and Maids, decided that somehow blacks needed to get the president's attention. In 1941, he proposed a march on Washington. The NAACP voted to join the march.

When the president heard about the proposed march, he asked White and Randolph to meet with him. Roosevelt tried his best to persuade the two to call off the march. He feared that the march would end in trouble as southern-bred Washington police worked to keep order. "How many will march?" he asked. "About one hundred thousand," was White's answer. The president began to work at once on drafting an executive order. One week later, on June 25, 1941, the president issued Executive Order 8802, which banned discrimination and segregation in government agencies, ordered that antidiscrimination clauses be included in defense contracts, and created the Fair Employment Practices Commission (FEPC), which would investigate complaints of violations. After twenty-eight years, the segregation and discrimination instituted by President Woodrow Wilson in government offices finally had been abolished. The march was canceled. The FEPC lasted until the end of the war, when Congress denied it funding. But the FEPC became the model for fair employment ordinances passed by cities across the nation in the early 1950s.

In the meantime, things were not going well with the pledges the president had made about the armed services. By 1943, a frustrated William Hastie had resigned his position as civilian aide to the secretary of war. He had worked very hard to see that blacks were allowed to enter all branches of the service, but the navy was making no effort to enlist blacks. The air corps had enlisted 2,500 blacks, whom they formed into ten aviation squadrons. These black airmen were sent to different airfields, but they had no special training or assignment, and the airfield commanders put them to work at menial chores in mess halls, hospitals, and barracks. Public and presidential pressure eventually forced the air corps to enlist blacks for aviation cadet training. However, rather than admitting them to the training facilities where white pilots were training, the air force built a base for black pilots in Tuskegee, Alabama.

Said Hastie, "There are none so blind as those who do not want to see. The air force command just does not want to see the advantages of training white and colored flyers together. I believe this blindness will continue until public criticism and condemnation of the segregated training policy becomes so strong that it can no longer be ignored."[18]

At the time of Hastie's resignation, the situation for black troops in Europe was discouraging. There were fights between black and white soldiers. Camps were segregated. Black soldiers, regardless of their

ability or education, were given assignments as stevedores, janitors, and truckers. White soldiers boarded
troop ships to the tune of "God Bless America," while
the band played "Dark Town Strutters Ball" for black
troops headed off to the war zone. For the most part,
blacks were kept out of combat, causing whites to call
them cowards.

NAACP executive director Walter White decided
to travel to the war zones to investigate the situation
for the NAACP and do what he could to alleviate the
problems he found. He applied to the War Department
for permission to go overseas, travel wherever he
chose, and interview whomever he wished. He finally
received permission to travel as a war correspondent.
White left for England in January 1944. When White
arrived in London, he found himself the focus of questions from other war correspondents, who wanted to
know if he was a White House spy. White believed that
this story had been given to the press by the War Department. With the label of White House spy, he certainly would have trouble traveling freely.

However, shortly after he arrived in London,
White was invited to dinner by Major General John C.
H. Lee. Most of the senior officers who reported to Lee
were also invited. Lee described to White what he
viewed as a dangerous situation of friction among
white and black troops, a situation impeding the progress of preparing for the invasion of the Normandy
coast in France—the invasion of Europe by Allied
forces to be mounted to move on Germany's forces.
The friction and the segregation were also shaming
the United States in the eyes of the British authorities,
who feared that U.S. bigotry against blacks would
spread to their country. Lee asked White to investigate
and make recommendations to correct the problems
he found. He told his officers that White was to have

full access to the U.S. installations in England, North Africa, and Italy.

White began a tour of the U.S.-held theater of war. He found that where there was trouble, the problem for the most part lay with white officers. In the officers' clubs, White, a light-skinned black often mistaken for white, overheard scores of bigoted statements not only about blacks but also about Jews, Catholics, and the people who lived in the country where the men were stationed.

In Naples, White noticed billboards throughout the city that said in Italian that blacks were "inferior human beings." The billboards threatened death by machine gun for any Italian woman who even spoke to a black soldier. It was signed "Italian American Committee for the Preservation of the Italian Race." White talked to the Italian authorities, who emphatically denied posting the billboards. When White spoke to the major general in charge of the Mediterranean theater, the general ordered an investigation, which revealed that the culprit was a U.S. Army colonel. He and the two sergeants who helped him were court-martialed. The effort to spread racial bigotry among Italians was reminiscent of the incident in France during World War I.

White officers used the power of their authority to make life miserable for black soldiers. Walter White discovered case after case of unjustly harsh punishment. One private was court-martialed for being minutes late for bed check. Blacks who complained about discrimination were court-martialed. In North Africa, when a group of black soldiers brought grievances of discrimination to their commanding officer, he cursed them and called them "niggers." He punished them by assigning them to malaria-control duty. A black soldier who protested this situation to General Eisenhower was court-martialed for going over his commanding officer's head.

Later that year, when White returned to London, he met with Lee and General Dwight Eisenhower, the Supreme Allied Commander. The two generals found the information gathered by White very discouraging. At Eisenhower's request, White wrote a long report on the injustices that he saw in Europe, together with recommendations. Some of the more unjust court-martial cases were corrected. Antidiscrimination orders were issued. But the fact remained that the white officers were key to the situation. If they were prejudiced and ignored the orders, life could be miserable for black soldiers.

In one case, the pressure of battle caused the U.S. Army to bend its segregation rule and give black soldiers a chance to prove themselves in combat. In the Belgian Ardennes Forest, the Germans were getting the best of the Allies at the Battle of the Bulge. Reinforcements were needed. A call for combat volunteers went out to black service and supply units. Black soldiers working as stevedores and warehousemen rushed to volunteer. In one unit, 171 out of 186 men volunteered. The black platoons fought bravely beside white platoons, pushing back the Germans. Black troops moved on to help win more battles. A few black soldiers received Distinguished Service Crosses, Silver Stars, and other medals.

An army poll of the troops produced good evidence that integration would not produce trouble among the troops. After joining black troops in combat, 77 percent of the white troops approved of integration, compared with 33 percent who favored integration beforehand. One South Carolina sergeant said that he had felt ashamed to wear the same shoulder patch as black soldiers but had changed his mind when he saw their bravery and skill in combat. "They are just like any of the other boys to us," he said.[19] Eighty percent of white officers and noncommissioned officers agreed that black soldiers had fought well. The NAACP believed that this was just the break needed to get the government to integrate the army. But neither the president nor Congress saw it that way. After victory was won in Europe, black troops were ordered back to their assignments in warehouses and on loading docks.

In the South Pacific, where he traveled in 1945, White found many of the same injustices he had seen in Europe, including many unjust court-martial verdicts. Through a telegram to the secretary of war, White managed to get the conviction of sixty-seven court-martialed black soldiers overturned. The soldiers had refused an order to "fall in" to formation by an abusive racist white officer.

On Guam, White was called upon to defend forty-four black sailors in a court-martial. The most serious charges against the sailors, who manned a navy supply depot, were rioting and attempted murder. For many weeks the men had been subject to name calling and harassment by a marine unit also stationed on Guam. The marines had even tossed live grenades into the camp of the black sailors. The blacks reported the attacks to their commanding officers, who did little or nothing to find the attackers or protect the sailors. The black sailors felt that it was up to them to protect themselves.

On Christmas Day, 1944, a marine had shot and killed a black sailor. A white sailor shot and seriously wounded a black sailor. Neither of the white servicemen was arrested. Finally, on Christmas night, a jeep drove into the black camp, spattering the area with machine gun fire. At this point, the black sailors became hysterically frightened, ready to attack anything they saw. When an MP jeep drove into the camp, the blacks fired on it, injuring one of the two MPs. As a group of forty-four black sailors set out in two trucks toward the marine camp, they were arrested and put in the brig.

Despite the fact that he was not a lawyer, White was asked to defend the forty-four sailors. White felt he could not agree to this. It did not seem just for the forty-four to be defended by someone who was not a lawyer. He could see that his participation would put the NAACP's seal of approval on the outcome. But the pleading look of the accused men, conveying their feeling of abandonment and friendlessness on an island full of hostile whites, made him change his mind.

Although the judge advocate had an assistant and access to navy records, White had neither. He had to do his own investigation and search for witnesses after the daily hearings ended. White lost the case, and the forty-four men were sentenced to prison terms. White later took the cases to the secretary of the navy and the president and succeeded in getting the convictions overturned.

At Pearl Harbor, White met with Fleet Admiral Chester Nimitz. Once more White brought up the matter of segregation in the navy and assigning blacks to serve in the mess. Nimitz said that he feared the effects of blacks outranking whites in peacetime. "But now we are at war. That's a different story," said Nimitz, apparently believing that the need for teamwork in battle would prevent racial tension. Nimitz invited White to tour a ship manned by a mixed crew of blacks and whites. White visited the ship and found it to be completely integrated.

Toward the end of the war, the secretaries of the navy and air force issued orders to enlist blacks into the navy and air force. But as the war ended, the armed services were for the most part still segregated, and discrimination still existed. In 1947, the President's Committee on Civil Rights found that "discrimination is one of the major elements which keeps the services from attaining the objectives which they have set for themselves." The committee found that fewer than one in seventy blacks was a commissioned officer; for whites the ratio was one to seven, ten times as high. In the navy, 80 percent of black sailors were cooks and stewards; only 2 percent of white sailors had similar assignments. Almost half of all white enlisted marines were in the three highest grades; less than 3 percent of all black enlisted marines held these three highest grades.[20]

At President Truman's request, White spoke to the heads of the military services, and he found them all determined to accomplish complete integration in the services. Finally, on July 26, 1948, the president issued an executive order calling for "equality of treatment and opportunity for all persons in the armed services without regard to race, color, religion, or national origin." Congress attempted but failed to pass a law that would have continued segregation in the armed services. In 1950, when the Korean War broke out, the armed services began to see and feel the full effects of integration. A white officer said of a black officer, "Because of him and other colored officers, I have changed my feelings about colored troops."[21] A white sergeant, speaking of his black lieutenant, said, "If he gave me an order, I would just have to do the job because I know it would come from higher headquarters."[22] Said a white GI, "The first night, we were drinking out of the same canteen cups. We treated them like all the other guys."[23]

White hoped that as white and black servicemen, so long separated by government and generals, came to understand one another, understanding would spread to their relationships in civilian life.

IX

THE GREAT DEBATE

At its founding, the NAACP set its sights on securing equality for black people in the voting booth, in the classroom, and in public places through the courts, the law, and the pressure of public opinion. But through the years, the organization would continue to be pressured to deal with the matter of helping poor blacks with their social and economic troubles—helping them find jobs, get health care, in short, survive. The NAACP would continue to insist that fighting for civil rights in the courts and the halls of Congress was the best way to help black people.

Founding member Mary Ovington wondered about the word "advancement" in the name of the organization. She wrote, "What direction did our advancement program take?" To Ovington, a social worker by profession, advancement meant many things in terms of helping black people. Beyond voting and education, the word applied to social problems such as family counseling, to income assistance as well as to employment.[1]

Six months after the NAACP was formed, George Haynes, a Fisk University sociologist, came into the NAACP office with an idea for a new organization to help blacks with employment and social problems. The Committee on Urban Conditions among Negroes would focus on the problems of blacks migrating from the rural South to cities. The committee would help rural blacks find jobs, housing, and education and assist them in adapting to city life. The organization would later merge with three other organizations to become the National Urban League.

"We gasped at having so large a field of advancement taken out of our program," said Ovington. The NAACP, which dared to work for the civil rights of blacks, was considered a militant organization in its early years. Ovington realized that such a militant organization as the NAACP would have trouble raising money for social services, and she knew that finding jobs for people was a full-time activity. "Nothing could have been more fortunate," said Ovington. The two organizations divided up the problems faced by black people, but they would occasionally join forces on an important project.[2]

But the informal agreement to split the problems did not settle the matter of the economic issue for the NAACP. By the 1930s, the nation was in deep economic trouble, and black people were getting the worst of it. In 1933, Urban League statistics showed that 17 percent of blacks existed on relief or welfare. At least half of the black urban population was on relief. Half of the black men living in large cities were out of work. In the South, discrimination kept blacks from even getting relief. Two-thirds of southern blacks who relied on cotton farming got little or no money for their efforts. An Urban League official called the economic and social outlook for the black "discouraging."

In the midst of this crisis, the NAACP made some

efforts to alleviate the economic distress of blacks. Funds were provided to assist the Southern Tenant Farmers Union. An unsuccessful effort was made to get the American Federation of Labor to require its member unions to admit black workers. The NAACP was successful in eliminating discrimination in the Public Works Administration, a New Deal program instituted by President Roosevelt in the midst of the Depression. The NAACP also worked to get fair wages for blacks working in the Works Progress Administration, another New Deal relief program.

However, at this point, many young educated blacks were openly criticizing the NAACP, arguing that it lacked an organized program for helping poverty-stricken blacks. The NAACP decided to invite some of the young black leaders to attend a conference "to discuss the present situation of the Negro in America."[3] "We hoped that a new view of the Negro's future and new programs would emerge," said Roy Wilkins, the NAACP assistant director.[4] The NAACP was looking for new ideas, but the conference would not be limited to what the NAACP should or should not do.

The Second Amenia Conference, like the first conference, was held in Amenia, New York, in August 1933 at Troutbeck, the estate of NAACP president Joel Spingarn. Thirty-three people attended the meeting—social workers, college professors, teachers, lawyers, librarians, physicians, and authors.

Although the conference produced no wealth of new ideas, it did force the NAACP to take a hard look at itself. The major idea that emerged from the three-day conference was a proposal that the NAACP work to bring white and black workers together into one labor movement that would serve as a power bloc to secure decent wages, benefits, and other rights for blacks and whites.

To W. E. B. DuBois, editor of *The Crisis,* the integrated labor union idea seemed unworkable because it meant that "white labor masses were supposed to accept without great reluctance the new scientific argument that there was no such thing as race." DuBois was disappointed that the conference did not support what he deemed a necessity: that blacks, segregated as they were, should work together to build their own businesses, banks, farms, and other economic institutions, giving them "self-support and social uplift. . . . From this haven of economic security, they could be even more effective in fighting discrimination," he said.[5]

In January 1934, DuBois made his idea the subject of a *Crisis* editorial. The editorial began with the words "The thinking colored people of the United States must stop being stampeded by the word segregation. The opposition to racial segregation is not or should not be any distaste or unwillingness of colored people to work with each other, to cooperate with each other, to live with each other. . . . [T]here should never be opposition to segregation pure and simple unless that segregation does involve discrimination." DuBois went on to suggest that blacks should form groups of communities and farms and should organize their own businesses: "It is the race-conscious black man cooperating together in his own institutions and movements who will eventually emancipate the colored race."[6]

In the days that followed, DuBois's editorial set off a flurry of angry responses by NAACP officials. Roy Wilkins saw this retreat to segregation as a retreat to Booker T. Washington's beliefs, strongly opposed by DuBois and the newly formed NAACP.[7] NAACP lawyer William H. Hastie said that while there can be segregation without unequal treatment, "any black man who uses this theoretical possibility as a justification for segregation is either dumb or mentally dishonest."[8]

The war of words continued in the pages of *The Crisis*. In the February issue, DuBois wrote an editorial supporting his point. "The NAACP has never officially opposed separate Negro organizations such as churches, schools, businesses, and cultural organizations," he wrote. "It has never denied the recurrent necessity of united separate action on the part of Negroes for self-defense and self-development," he said, pointing out that separate action is a necessary evil.[9]

NAACP officials responded in the March 1934 edition of *The Crisis*. NAACP president Joel Spingarn wrote: "We were always against segregation, we always regarded it as an evil, if sometimes a necessary evil. The association has never accepted the distinction between discrimination and segregation which Dr. DuBois makes in his January editorial. We felt that where there was segregation there must always inevitably be discrimination. Even voluntary segregation is an evil."[10] Executive Secretary Walter White added, "In a world where time and space are being demolished by science, it is no longer possible to create or imagine separate racial, national, or other compartments of human thought and endeavor. The Negro must without yielding, continue the grim struggle for integration and against segregation for his own physical, moral, and spiritual well-being."[11]

In his April editorial, DuBois wrote, "All Negroes agree that segregation is bad . . . but if they live in the United States in 1934 . . . they are segregated. What is the Negro going to do?" He must make sure "that segregation does not harm his health and well-being. . . . If he cannot educate his children in decent schools, he must nevertheless educate his children in decent Negro schools and arrange and conduct and oversee such schools. If he cannot enter American industry at a living wage or find work suited to his education and talent, or receive promotion or advancement according to his deserts, he must organize his own economic life." DuBois saw this tactic as not only necessary but inevitable.[12]

The May issue of *The Crisis* carried the text of a resolution passed by the NAACP board: "The NAACP is opposed both to the principle and the practice of enforced segregation of human beings on the basis of race and color. Enforced segregation by its very existence carries with it the implication of a superior and inferior group and invariably results in the imposition of a lower status on the group deemed inferior."[13]

DuBois countered with "It would be interesting to know what the board means by the resolution." His editorial went on to cite the twenty-six thousand black churches, the many black colleges, the two hundred black newspapers, as well as black business, history, spirituals, art, and literature. "And if it does not believe in these things, is the board of directors of the NAACP afraid to say so?" he wrote.[14]

DuBois believed strongly that times had changed since 1909, when the NAACP was founded, and that in 1934, it must change its program to meet the needs of most blacks, who had no work, little money, and inadequate education: the legal program had to give way to an economic program. He believed that the NAACP in the late 1920s and early 1930s had attracted well-to-do blacks who wanted to fight social discrimination rather than work for the status and power of blacks as a group. He was convinced that as far as the NAACP was concerned, policy aimed at effecting economic change and organization among black people was out of the question. "I began to see that for the second time in my life, my occupation was gone," he said.[15]

On June 26, 1934, he sent his letter of resignation to the NAACP. "Today this organization which has been great and effective for nearly a quarter of a century finds itself in a time of crisis and change without a program. My program for economic readjustment has been totally ignored.... I personally can do no more.... I am insisting on my resignation on July 1." He ended by wishing the organization well and indicating that he was ready to applaud it "when it is able to rescue itself from its present impossible position and reorganize itself according to the demands of the present crisis."[16]

DuBois was unaware that even as he wrote his resignation, the board was discussing ways to do just what he had urged—address the current economic problems of black people. The Future Plan and Program committee, headed by black economist Abram Harris, was formed and charged with studying the Second Amenian resolutions. The Harris committee submitted its report for a new NAACP economic program in September 1934. The report called for an educational program that emphasized the problems shared by both black and white workers. It described methods for bringing black and white workers together into a power bloc and recommended research into industrial and agricultural economics.

The report also called for establishing an economic affairs committee made up of professional economists, to direct the program with little or no direction from the board or the national office. The Harris committee would implement its new program through reorganization of the branches, making their programs and projects more appealing to working-class blacks.

For nearly a year, the board and the national office wrangled over the Harris committee plan, taking this idea out, removing that element, until the result scarcely resembled the proposed plan. Still, there were objections. The new economic program would cost too much. It would not appeal to the whites and middle-

class black who were the principal financial supporters of the NAACP. It could subject the NAACP and
blacks to being labeled radicals or Socialists, increasing racism. Finally, in the fall of 1935, the plan was
abandoned.

For the next twenty-five years, the NAACP continued to pursue civil rights in courtrooms, halls of Congress, and Oval Office. Then, in the early 1960s, the
NAACP endured another assault on its relationship
with the ordinary black person. In 1954, the NAACP
had succeeded in winning a Supreme Court decision in
Brown v. *Board of Education* that said separate is not
equal, that segregation is against the law. The decision
was a moment of triumph for the organization, but it
also bitterly demonstrated the limits of the NAACP's
litigation program. Blacks believed that the Supreme
Court decision would produce instant desegregation,
that segregation was ended, that they would be free to
sit where they pleased on buses, eat in restaurants,
and enjoy full rights. But the import of the Supreme
Court decision had not reached the typical bus company or restaurant proprietor in the South. The
"whites only" signs stayed up. The NAACP conceiv-
ably would have had to argue a case in court against
every defiant town, perhaps against every defiant bus
company and lunch counter to force the issue and end
segregation.

Impatient for their rights, blacks could not wait for
those hundreds of court decisions. They stepped forward to take that seat on the bus or that stool at the
lunch counter. Across the South, blacks "sat in" at
lunch counters enduring insults and plates of spoiled
food. Everyday, blacks returned to sit at the counter,
delivering the message: "We have a right to be here.
We are as good as whites." Finally, they won the right
to be served at the counter. Blacks persisted in regis-
tering to vote. Joining with white supporters, they

filled integrated buses that were often attacked and set afire by angry bigots as they pulled into local bus stations. Watching all of this on television, Americans saw a horrifying image of themselves. One by one the walls of segregation collapsed.

The 1960s were a violent but productive time for blacks. Some died violently, many were arrested, but they got those seats on the bus and at the lunch counter. They became voters.

Many blacks called for separatism and black power, while others turned to nonviolence and prayer in the streets. It was a strange and bewildering time for the NAACP, the civil rights pioneer accustomed to pursuing the problems of racism in meetings and courtrooms and pamphlets.

Many blacks called the NAACP soft and narrow. Soft meant it was not hard-hitting and fearless because it looked to its white backers for approval of its actions. Narrow referred once more to the charge heard during the 1934 debate with DuBois that the organization was not concerning itself with the needs of poor blacks.[17]

Blacks and whites constantly compared the NAACP with newer organizations such as the Student Non-Violent Coordinating Committee (SNCC). One Mississippi NAACP branch official, bemoaning the fact that he had "to move according to the law," called in SNCC to run a voter registration drive that would help and encourage black voters to register. SNCC, he said, was the only thing "that gave courage and determination" to southern blacks.[18]

Medgar Evers, the NAACP branch official in Jackson, Mississippi, felt that the NAACP's legal program was outdated and that the organization needed to change its approach. In the late 1950s, he had tried unsuccessfully to get the national office to endorse sit-ins and other strategies that would produce immediate results.[19]

Roy Wilkins, the NAACP executive director, began to feel Evers's impatience himself. Finally, in March 1960, he ordered the branches to support sit-ins. To send a strong message, he gathered the entire staff of the New York City national office and picketed two stores—Woolworths and Kresges—around the corner from the office. The pickets carried signs that demanded that the stores direct their southern branches to serve blacks at their lunch counters. The NAACP also paid many a bond for young activists arrested during demonstrations. Wilkins had made moves to bring his organization closer to the masses, to the gut issues of people reaching for their rights.

In the summer of 1960, as the NAACP convention was about to begin, Wilkins's support of the sit-ins worried some NAACP officials. They feared that the young delegates, most of whom were veterans of sit-ins and voter-registration drives, would take over the convention and run out the old guard and their programs, too. Wilkins didn't know what to expect when he entered one meeting hall filled with young delegates. He announced that the latest sit-in effort had integrated some Virginia stores. Cheers filled the room, and two students lifted Wilkins up on their shoulders and proceeded to carry him around the room to the resounding laughter and whoops of the students.

Then suddenly, the laughter and cheers stopped. NAACP president Arthur Spingarn, an NAACP founder, had entered the room. Spingarn knew he was witnessing a changing and dynamic NAACP. His eyes filled with tears as he said, "I thank God for what I have lived to see." He commended the young people and Wilkins for their intelligence, courage, and resolve. "Don't stop," he said. The NAACP was changing, reaching out to all blacks with help and support for the everyday, gritty problems of being black in America.

It would be Benjamin Hooks, a public defender, a minister, a judge, and a former member of the Federal Communications Commission, who would lead the NAACP in that direction. In 1977, he succeeded Wilkins as executive director.

X

A TALK WITH
BEN HOOKS[1]

Benjamin Hooks' graying hair lent the aura of aging to this man of sixty-five. But something about his steady, direct gaze that told you this was the face of a man with young ideas. This was a leader who for fifteen years directed over three hundred thousand NAACP members across the country in the achievement of countless victories for black people.

Now, as he contemplated retirement, Hooks thought back to 1949 when, fresh out of Chicago's DePaul University law school, he returned to his hometown of Memphis, a place where black people certainly had much need for victories. "There were 'colored' bathrooms, 'colored' drinking fountains. We could not choose any seat in a movie theater as we can now. We had to use separate entrances and sit in the third balcony. Some of the theaters wouldn't let us in at all. You would get discourteous treatment from the man pumping gas. We couldn't stay in hotels north or south. I've been turned down so many times," he says, shaking his head sadly.

"Everywhere you looked we were left out. I was not allowed to use the law library. You could walk through the courthouse and never see a black person typing or collecting taxes. You never saw a black policeman or bank teller. There were just no jobs where you could wear a coat and tie. Black people were maids or janitors. It was rigid, unyielding segregation. There was so much hatefulness," he said, meeting a visitor's gaze with a doleful look.

Hooks pondered the role of the NAACP in changing that picture. "Take affirmative action, for example. It opened doors for hundreds of thousands of black people in all kinds of jobs that they take for granted today.

"Yes, Rosa Parks sat on the bus in Montgomery, but it was a NAACP suit that won the day for the Montgomery bus boycotters. We had been working on bus segregation for a while. We had been doing what we called test cases. About two hundred people all across the country took seats in the front of buses and found themselves in court for that offense. Finally, we got these cases as one consolidated case on the Supreme Court calendar. And on the very day that the city of Montgomery was about to come out with an ordinance that would have made jitneys, or private taxis, illegal, the Supreme Court decision came through. The boycotters were relying on the jitneys to get to work. The Supreme Court decision said that you could not have separate seating on buses.

"We've marched and demonstrated, too. In fact, Roy Wilkins told me that eighty percent of the young people arrested in the South in the sixties were NAACP people—supporters or members. You can march, but you've got to have a plan, a strategy. You've got to lobby, help write laws. We spent many long weeks, days, hours— planning, strategizing just how to outwit our opponents. We had lawyers like Thurgood

Marshall who won twenty-nine out of the thirty-one cases he argued before the Supreme Court. No one else has ever done that.

"Marching is catalytic. It builds your spirit and it builds support. It gets attention for the cause. It calls attention to the law you're proposing.

"I remember we managed to overturn one law that said practically anybody could be arrested for loitering or vagrancy. NAACP lawyers made it illegal to arrest someone for loitering on trumped-up, vague charges. That's an achievement that helped everybody—black and white.

"And we did some of the first sit-ins. In 1927, NAACP member Bishop William Wells of the African Methodist Episcopal Church sat down in the restaurant in Washington's Union Station and wouldn't leave until they served him. And for many years, up into the fifties, that was the only place in Washington where blacks and whites could eat together."

As he considered the recent activity of the NAACP, Hooks feared that history was being repeated in the actions of the Supreme Court. He noted that the high court was doing to blacks what it did in the 1870s— overturning the effects of civil rights acts passed by Congress. He pointed out that since 1989, the high court had done so in seven or eight different cases.

And now came President George Bush's veto of the 1990 Civil Rights Act. "What hypocrisy, claiming that the act calls for quotas in hiring. It's got nothing to do with quotas, but even if it did, what's so bad about that. A quota is like a timetable, a goal. Pay what you owe, meet the deadline. Black people are owed an opportunity for employment."

What this meant, said Hooks, was that NAACP lawyers couldn't let up in their efforts. They had to continue to help blacks who were unfairly convicted and tried for crimes. They had to file cases involving segregated housing, education, and discrimination in voting and employment.

Since the early 1980s, the NAACP has found it necessary to develop programs to deal with the painful economic and social problems that blacks face. It is an effort that has been urged on the organization since the days of DuBois's editorials and the Second Amenia conference. Hooks noted, "In those days, segregation and discrimination were so hateful and unyielding that it was necessary to devote all our resources to getting laws and Supreme Court rulings that guaranteed blacks their civil rights." But now, apparently, the NAACP felt the reverse was true.

In 1980, 40 percent of black children belonged to poor families, compared with 11 percent of white children. In that year, the NAACP adopted its Policy Statement on the Economic Well-Being of Blacks, which describes strategies to deal with the economic plight of black families. The basic strategies are challenging job discrimination, assisting black people in dealing with their environment, and shaping and molding factors such as education and experience, which affect income. The NAACP established an Economic Development Department.

Said Hooks, "We wanted to make certain that blacks got their fair share of the economic pie, that they got hired at the entry level, that they were promoted to management and senior level positions, that companies put minority vendor programs in place to give black-owned companies an equal chance to sell their supplies and services. We also felt that companies should elect blacks to their boards and donate money to black causes. We developed a program to encourage these things, which we call Fair Share. So far we have signed Fair Share Agreements with about fifty companies, companies like General Motors, K

Mart, Disney Studios, MGM, Hardee's, Coors, and McDonald's.

"The Act-So program inspires black youth to achieve by creating an arena in which they can compete in fields such as architecture, chemistry, computer science, electronics, mathematics, physics, painting, music, and writing. So far about thirty thousand youths have participated. We also have a Back to School/Stay in School program, which works with students and parents to encourage youngsters to get an education."

At the NAACP's 80th annual convention in 1989, delegates adopted a number of resolutions that focused on other economic issues:

- To support the Smart Start Act being considered by Congress that would establish an early-childhood education program.
- To work for legislation to strengthen small businesses, particularly those in black communities.
- To work for the establishment of an American Development Bank to fund the revitalization of blighted urban areas and to serve as a financial management advisor to such urban business-people.
- To urge Congress to adopt requirements that state and local governments and their contractors hire more blacks for highway construction.

Addressing the delegates to the 81st NAACP Annual Convention, Hooks called for a "commitment to saving our less fortunate brothers and sisters—locked in poverty and despair. If we allow a third of black America to wallow in poverty, allow black men to continue to be gunned down at alarming rates, watch our people become intoxicated by the lures of the drug trade, history will embarrass us. . . . If we allow the so-called black underclass to languish, history will record us as the first generation that left black America worse off than when we found it. . . .

"Can we not do more for ourselves? Certainly. . . . That is why the NAACP is calling together a summit conference of major black organizations to address the flood of problems that are destroying our community and weakening us as a people."

Members of 100 black organizations came to the summit. Said Hooks, "These were the many strong and viable organizations within the African American community that have for years been putting forth remarkable efforts in seeking to stitch up the tattered fabric found in some sectors of their communities."

They came to share ideas that worked—to help a teenage mother, a child tempted by drugs, a black man without a job. For three days they attended workshops and plenary sessions. They planned a communications network for sharing ideas. They discussed ways to make the best use of people and money to help black communities. A brain trust to study the socioeconomic concerns of the black community was discussed. And they talked about projects that work, like the Kansas City Ad Hoc Group Against Crime, and the National Black Farmers' Harvest, and the Adopt-A-Class program initiated by Atlanta's One Hundred Black Men.

The delegates formed themselves into the National Association of Black Organizations and made Hooks their chairman. Hooks gave the group their marching orders: "We have a moral responsibility to attack the problems in our community with the best weapon at our disposal—black unity."

Hooks also kept a weather eye on that historic goal that has occupied the NAACP for more than eighty years: "To achieve for blacks the rights that whites take for granted. The NAACP is bringing black Americans out of subjugation, slavery, and second-class citizenship, and that lets all America hold up its head and be proud."

Did he think there would ever be a time when there was no need for an NAACP? "Not in my lifetime," Hooks said. "Racism is too prevalent. Look at the Mideast. They've been hating each other for 5,000 years—so long they don't know why they're hating. It's foolish to think racism could be eliminated in the hearts of men and women in America in ten . . . twenty . . . even a hundred years. Maybe my great-great-great-great-great granddaughter will see the day."

EPILOGUE

For this black American, the past few years spent working on this book have been a heartbreaking time. Day after day as I researched this book, the sorrowful facts accumulated—of the centuries-long humiliation, debasing, torture, and murder of darker-skinned Americans by other Americans. All I could think was "America, how could you?"

Some may say that black Americans have suffered these eons of injustice at the hands of a few hateful people. Not so. What we have here is a wrong, rooted in our political system. To exist and survive, segregation and discrimination, and yes, even lynching, had to be sanctioned by presidents, senators, state legislators, and town council members. The founders of the NAACP understood this and set out to challenge America's racial injustice in the courts and the halls of Congress. Now and then for the NAACP there was that stunning moment when a president or senator or an ordinary citizen stepped forward to join the fight to right the wrong. And that reveals a uniquely American quality. I call that quality constructive introspection—it looks at the America we have and says, "This is wrong. Let's fix it." That good old-fashioned American quality often made the difference for the NAACP.

You have read of the NAACP's painstaking efforts in courtroom and legislative session to right a wrong against the civil rights of a black person. And when victory was won and the court ruled in the black person's favor or a new law was signed, there wasn't time for celebration. The NAACP lawyers had to move on to deal with a loophole someone had devised to get around the decision or the law. The loophold devisers reasoned if the grandfather clause is made illegal, then let's deny blacks the right to vote in primaries. If housing segregation laws are overturned, let's try restrictive covenants. Going after the loopholes demonstrates the most remarkable quality of the NAACP—patience, resourcefulness, dogged determination to meet the foes of racial justice on their own terms.

Think what the NAACP has accomplished in some eighty years. Maybe if you're white, you take it for granted. But life is freer now for black people. We can stay in hotels, sit where we please on buses and in restaurants, get good jobs, go to the movies and theaters, buy houses. We see our images in the persons of movie stars, TV anchors, governors, mayors, congresspersons, generals—and our chests swell with pride. "I am somebody," we say.

It would be nice to say that we all lived happily ever after. But there is still racial injustice out there. And the NAACP fights on. Even after the order went out to desegregate schools, segregation continues. Through the 1980s and early 1990s, the NAACP has been working to desegregate schools in Cleveland, Columbus, Detroit, St. Louis, and Yonkers, New York. Long after President Truman signed his executive order to desegregate the armed services, the NAACP found itself obliged to file suits against racism at Florida's Eglin Air Force Base, the U.S. Air Force base at Goose Bay, Nova Scotia, army bases in West Germany, and the aircraft carrier *Kitty Hawk*. More loopholes to take on, even now. You can be sure the NAACP will be out there until that last loophole is defeated.

CHRONOLOGY

1863 On January 1, President Abraham Lincoln issues the Emancipation Proclamation.

1865 Congress passes the Thirteenth Amendment, which frees the slaves and abolishes slavery.

1866 Congress passes the Civil Rights Act of 1866, which forbids discrimination on account of race.

1868 Congress passes the Fourteenth Amendment, which makes the ex-slave a citizen.

1870 The Fifteenth Amendment is passed by Congress, giving ex-slaves the right to vote.

1871 Congress passes the Civil Rights Act of 1871, which is intended to protect black people from terrorist groups.

1875 Civil Rights Act of 1875 is passed, making discrimination against blacks a crime.

1883 Supreme Court declares two sections of the 1875 Civil Rights Act unconstitutional.

1896 In *Plessy* v. *Ferguson* the Supreme Court rules that "separate but equal" facilities do not violate the rights of black citizens, giving the high court's blessing to segregation.

1908 The Springfield, Illinois, race riot takes place in August.

1909 On February 12, Lincoln's birthday, *The Call*, urging people to address the wrongs suffered by black people, is issued.

1909 On May 31, the Negro National Conference meets to plan the organization that will become the NAACP.

1910 In May, the NAACP begins its campaign to get the vote for black people. The first issue of *The Crisis* is published in November.

1911 The NAACP is incorporated in the state of New York in May.

1913 Segregation of blacks and whites is instituted in federal government offices in Washington, D.C., setting an example for the nation.

1915 In February, black biologist Ernest Just is awarded the first NAACP Spingarn Medal.

In June, the NAACP achieves its first legal victory when the Supreme Court rules in *Guinn* v. *United States* that the use of the grandfather clause to qualify voters violates the Fifteenth Amendment.

1916 First Amenia Conference is called to bring together the Booker T. Washington and the NAACP civil rights factions.

1917 In June, the U.S. Department of War opens a separate training camp for black officers in Des Moines, Iowa. First class graduates in October.

In July, scores of black men, women, and children are killed in the East St. Louis race riot. In protest of the violence, ten thousand black people stage a "Silent March" down New York City's Fifth Avenue.

In August, black soldiers riot in Houston, Texas. One hundred twenty-four soldiers are arrested. Following trials, nineteen are hanged and the rest jailed. As a result of continuous NAACP appeals to the president, the last soldier is finally released from jail in 1938.

In November, the Supreme Court rules that segregated housing laws are unconstitutional.

1919 In April and May, W. E. B. DuBois investigates and reports in *The Crisis* on the racial injustices inflicted by the army on black troops serving overseas.

In May, the NAACP holds anti-lynching conference.

In June, NAACP membership is fifty-six thousand.

In June, the first incident of Red Summer, a summer of racial violence, begins in Longview, Texas.

In December, James Weldon Johnson becomes the first black NAACP executive secretary.

1922 In January, the NAACP-sponsored Dyer anti-lynching bill is passed by the House of Representatives. It is defeated in December after three-month Senate filibuster.

1926 The NAACP wins freedom for seventy-nine black men unjustly accused of murder and insurrection in Phillips County, Arkansas.

1927 The Supreme Court rules that blacks have the right to vote in primary elections.

1930 In May, the NAACP campaign to fight President Herbert Hoover's nomination of John J. Parker for judge achieves victory when the Senate rejects the nomination, marking the coming of age of the black voter.

1931 The Costigan-Wagner antilynching bill is defeated by a Senate filibuster.

1933 In August, the NAACP holds the Second Amenia Conference to discuss new ideas for helping black people.

1935 The NAACP wins a decision in a Maryland court of appeals, and the University of Maryland is ordered to admit a black student to its law school.

1940 The Wagner-Gavagan antilynching bill is defeated by Senate filibuster.

1941 The Supreme Court rules that denying black people sleeping and dining facilities on trains is unconstitutional.

On June 25, President Franklin Roosevelt issues Executive Order 8802, which bans discrimination in defense industries and establishes the Fair Employment Practices Commission. This action forestalls a march on Washington proposed by the NAACP and the Brotherhood of Sleeping Car Porters.

1944 NAACP-sponsored case wins a Supreme Court ruling that separate seating for blacks and whites on interstate buses is an undue burden to bus companies.

1947 In the fall, the Truman Commission on Civil Rights issues *To Secure These Rights,* which calls for twenty-seven different civil rights acts to secure the rights guaranteed to black people. The commission was formed as a result of a meeting between President Harry Truman and an NAACP committee.

The Supreme Court rules that the Fourteenth Amendment protects the property rights of blacks, and restrictive real estate covenants cannot be enforced.

1948 President Harry Truman issues an executive order that ends segregation in the armed services.

1950 The Supreme Court rules that black students cannot be segregated at the University of Oklahoma College of Education graduate school, stating that segregation would interfere with the student's opportunity to learn.

1950 In *Henderson* v. *United States,* the Supreme Court rules that racial segregation in dining cars is unconstitutional.

1954 On May 17, the Supreme Court rules in *Brown* v. *Board of Education* that "separate educational facilities are inherently unequal."

1957 Congress passes the Civil Rights Act of 1957, making it a federal crime to interfere with a citizen's right to vote.

1960 The Civil Rights Act of 1960 calls for federal supervision of voter registration.

1964 The Twenty-fourth Amendment to the Constitution, which abolishes the poll tax, is ratified by Congress.

Congress passes the Civil Rights Act of 1964, which calls for full voting rights, outlaws discrimination in public places and on the job, calls for funding to desegregate schools, and provides enforcement measures.

1965 Civil Rights Act of 1965 is passed. The Act strengthens voting rights measures, outlaws devices used by registrars to keep blacks from voting.

1968 Civil Rights Act of 1968, containing antiriot clauses and calling for open housing, is passed by Congress.

1980 NAACP adopts its Policy Statement on the Economic Well-Being of Blacks.

1982 The first Fair Share agreement is signed with the Edison Electric Institute and the American Gas Association, whose member companies would be urged to increase job opportunities for blacks.

1984 The NAACP and the Urban League sponsor a Black Family Summit Conference to address the contemporary problems of the black family.

1985 The NAACP board of directors approves the creation of a small-business incubator project.

The NAACP creates the Economic Development Corporation, a nonprofit subsidiary.

1990 The National Association of Black Organizations is formed to deal with the social and economic problems of blacks.

SOURCES

I

1. Frederick Douglas, "1852: What to the American Slave Is Your 4th of July?" *New York Times*, July 4, 1975, p. C23.

2. *Testimony Taken by the Joint Committee to Inquire into the Condition of Affairs in the Late Insurrectionary States— Mississippi*, vol. 1. (Washington, D.C.: Government Printing Office, 1872).

3. Alan Westin, *Freedom Now* (New York: Basic Books, 1964), pp. 72–73.

4. Ida B. Wells, *Crusade for Justice* (Chicago: University of Chicago Press, 197), p. 50.

II

1. James L. Crouthamel, "The Springfield Riot of 1908," *Journal of Negro History*, July 1960, p. 164.

2. Crouthamel, p. 177.

3. Crouthamel, p. 179.

4. Mary White Ovington, *The Walls Came Tumbling Down* (New York: Schocken, 1970), p. 102.

5. Charles Flint Kellogg, *NAACP—a History of the National Association for the Advancement of Colored People, 1909–1920* (Baltimore: Johns Hopkins University Press, 1967), p. 11.

6. Kellogg, p. 11.

7. Oswald Garrison Villard, *Fighting Years, Memoirs of a Liberal Editor* (New York: Harcourt Brace, 1939), p. 192.

8. Kellogg, p. 297.

9. Booker T. Washington, *Up from Slavery* (New York: Dodd Mead, 1965), p. 142.

10. Kellogg, p. 19.

11. Kellogg, p. 19.

12. Kellogg, p. 20.

13. Kellogg, p. 20.

14. Kellogg, p. 22.

15. Kellogg, p. 24.

16. Mary White Ovington, "Beginnings of the NAACP," *The Crisis,* June 1926, p. 77.

III

1. W. E. B. DuBois, *Dusk of Dawn* (New York: Harcourt Brace, 1940), p. 227.

2. Charles Flint Kellogg, *NAACP—a History of the National Association for the Advancement of Colored People, 1909–1920* (Baltimore: Johns Hopkins University Press, 1967), p. 92.

3. Kellogg, p. 93.

4. Kellogg, p. 93.

5. Kellogg, p. 52.

6. DuBois, p. 271.

7. "Reports of Branches," *The Crisis,* February 1914, p. 192.

8. Kellogg, p. 88.

9. James Weldon Johnson, *Along This Way* (New York: Viking, 1933), p. 314.

10. "Report on Membership," *The Crisis*, June 1919, p. 59.

IV

1. Mary White Ovington, *The Walls Came Tumbling Down* (New York: Schocken, 1970), p. 113.

2. Ovington, p. 112.

3. Albert E. Pillsbury, "A Federal Remedy for Lynching," *Harvard Law Review*, vol. 15, no. 9.

4. James Weldon Johnson, *Along This Way* (New York: Viking, 1933), p. 319.

5. Johnson, p. 321.

6. Johnson, p. 317.

7. Johnson, p. 327.

8. Charles Flint Kellogg, *NAACP—a History of the National Association for the Advancement of Colored People, 1909–1920* (Baltimore: Johns Hopkins University Press, 1967), p. 227.

9. Johnson, p. 329.

10. Ovington, p. 174–75.

11. Walter White, *A Man Called White* (New York: Doubleday, 1945), p. 46.

12. Johnson, p. 366.

13. Johnson, p. 369.

14. Johnson, p. 369.

15. Johnson, p. 373.

V

1. Charles Flint Kellogg, *NAACP—a History of the National Association for the Advancement of Colored People, 1909–1920* (Baltimore: Johns Hopkins University Press, 1967), p. 45.

2. Walter White, *How Far the Promised Land* (New York: Viking, 1955), p. 68.
3. White, p. 68.
4. Walter White, *A Man Called White* (New York: Doubleday, 1945), p. 89.
5. White, *A Man Called White,* p. 90.
6. White, *A Man Called White,* p. 105.
7. White, *A Man Called White,* p. 111.
8. White, *A Man Called White,* p. 263.
9. "Highlights of NAACP History 1909–1988," *The Crisis,* 80th Anniversary Issue, p. 92.

VI

1. Walter White, *How Far the Promised Land* (New York: Viking, 1955), p. 32.
2. Walter White, *A Man Called White* (New York: Doubleday, 1945), p. 45.
3. Augustus Low and Virgil A. Clift, editors, *Encyclopedia of Black America* (New York: Da Capo, 1981), p. 449.
4. "Highlights of NAACP History 1909–1988," *The Crisis,* 80th Anniversary Issue, p. 94.
5. "Highlights of NAACP History 1909–1988," p. 97.
6. Low and Clift, editors, *Encyclopedia of Black America,* p. 450.

VII

1. Mark V. Tushnet, *The NAACP's Legal Strategy against Segregated Education, 1925–50* (Chapel Hill: University of North Carolina Press, 1987), p. 34.
2. Tushnet, p. 132.
3. Tushnet, p. 135.
4. "History of the Five School Cases," *The Crisis,* June–July 1954, p. 338.

5. "Text of United States Supreme Court Decision Outlawing Negro Segregation in the Public Schools," *The Crisis,* June–July 1954, p. 327.

6. "Editorials—Segregation Decision," *The Crisis,* June–July 1954, p. 352.

7. "Along the NAACP Battlefront," *The Crisis,* June–July 1954, p. 359.

8. "Nation's Press on Segregation Ruling," *The Crisis,* June–July 1954, p. 348.

9. "Nation's Press on Segregation Ruling," pp. 347–48.

10. Augustus Low and Virgil A. Clift, editors, *Encyclopedia of Black America* (New York: Da Capo, 1981), p. 254.

VIII

1. Charles Flint Kellogg, *NAACP—a History of the National Association for the Advancement of Colored People, 1909–1920* (Baltimore: Johns Hopkins University Press, 1967), p. 159.

2. Kellogg, p. 162.

3. "Editorials—The President," *The Crisis,* February 1915, p. 181.

4. Kellogg, *NAACP,* p. 253.

5. Kellogg, p. 255.

6. Kellogg, p. 255.

7. "Editorials," *The Crisis,* June 1917, p. 60.

8. Mary White Ovington, *The Walls Came Tumbling Down* (New York: Schocken, 1970), p. 134.

9. "The History of the Black Man," *The Crisis,* June 1919, p. 71.

10. "The History of the Black Man," p. 69.

11. "The History of the Black Man," p. 71.

12. "Opinion: Rape," *The Crisis,* May 1919, p. 12.

13. W. E. B. DuBois, "Documents of the War," *The Crisis,* May 1919, pp. 16–17.

14. "The History of the Black Man," p. 78.

15. "The Brave Son," *The Crisis,* March 1919, p. 222.

16. Walter White, *A Man Called White* (New York: Doubleday, 1945), p. 188.

17. White, p. 188.

18. Walter White, *How Far the Promised Land* (New York: Viking, 1955), p. 92.

19. White, *A Man Called White,* p. 250.

20. White, *How Far the Promised Land,* p. 94.

21. White, *How Far the Promised Land,* p. 99.

22. White, *How Far the Promised Land,* p. 101.

23. White, *How Far the Promised Land,* p. 102.

IX

1. Mary White Ovington, *The Walls Came Tumbling Down* (New York: Schocken, 1970), p. 111.

2. Ovington, p. 112.

3. Roy Wilkins, *Standing Fast* (New York: Viking, 1982), p. 151.

4. Wilkins, p. 151.

5. W. E. B. DuBois, *Dusk of Dawn* (New York: Harcourt Brace, 1940), p. 301.

6. W. E. B. DuBois, "Postscript: Segregation," *The Crisis,* January 1934, p. 20.

7. Wilkins, *Standing Fast,* p. 152.

8. Wilkins, pp. 152–53.

9. W. E. B. DuBois, "Postscript: The NAACP and Race Segregation," *The Crisis,* February 1934, p. 53.

10. J. E. Spingarn, "Segregation—a Symposium," *The Crisis,* March 1934, p. 79.

11. Walter White, "Segregation—a Symposium," *The Crisis,* March 1934, p. 81.

12. W. E. B. DuBois, "Postscript: Objects of Segregation," *The Crisis,* April 1934, p. 116.

13. W. E. B. DuBois, "Postscript: The Board of Directors on Segregation," *The Crisis,* May 1934, p. 149.

14. DuBois, *Dusk of Dawn,* p. 149.

15. DuBois, *Dusk of Dawn,* p. 302.

16. "Dr. DuBois Resigns," *The Crisis,* August 1934, p. 245.

17. Robert Penn Warren, *Who Speaks for the Negro* (New York: Random House, 1965), p. 145.

18. Henry Hampton and Steve Fayer, *Voices of Freedom* (New York: Bantam, 1990), p. 141.

19. Hampton and Fayer, p. 151.

X

1. Interview with Benjamin Hooks, August 17 1990, Washington, D.C.

BIBLIOGRAPHY

Angle, Paul M. *A Pictorial History of the Civil War Years.* New York: Doubleday, 1967.

DuBois, W. E. B. *Dusk of Dawn.* New York: Harcourt Brace, 1940.

Hampton, Henry, and Steve Fayer. *Voices of Freedom.* New York: Bantam, 1990.

Jackson, W. Sherman. *The Lost Promise: Reconstruction in the South.* Middletown, Conn.: Xerox Corporation, 1971.

Johnson, James Weldon. *Along This Way.* New York: Viking, 1933.

Kellogg, Charles Flint. *NAACP—a History of the National Association for the Advancement of Colored People, 1909–1920.* Baltimore: Johns Hopkins University Press, 1967.

Low, Augustus, and Virgil A. Clift, editors. *Encyclopedia of Black America.* New York: Da Capo, 1981.

Ovington, Mary White. *The Walls Came Tumbling Down.* New York: Schocken, 1970.

Rivlin, Benjamin, editor. *Ralph Bunche, the Man and His Times.* New York: Holmes and Meier, 1990.

Tushnet, Mark V. *The NAACP's Legal Strategy against Segregated Education, 1925–50.* Chapel Hill: University of North Carolina Press, 1987.

Villard, Oswald Garrison. *Fighting Years: Memoirs of a Liberal Editor.* New York: Harcourt Brace, 1939.

Warren, Robert Penn. *Who Speaks for the Negro.* New York: Random House, 1965.

Washington, Booker T. *Up from Slavery.* New York: Dodd Mead, 1965.

Westin, Alan. *Freedom Now.* New York: Basic Books, 1964.

White, Walter. *A Man Called White.* New York: Doubleday, 1945.

White, Walter. *How Far the Promised Land.* New York: Viking, 1955.

Wilkins, Roy. *Standing Fast.* New York: Viking, 1982.

Williams, T. Harry. *The Life History of the United States 1849–1865.* New York: Time-Life Books, 1963.

Williams, T. Harry. *The Life History of the United States 1861–1876.* New York: Time-Life Books, 1964.

FOR FURTHER READING

Bontemps, Arna. *100 Years of Negro Freedom.* New York: Dodd, 1961.

Douglas, Frederick. *1817–1895: Life and Times of Frederick Douglas, Written by Himself.* Secaucus, N.J.: Citadel Press, 1983.

Fraser, Alison. *Walter White.* New York: Chelsea House, 1991.

Hamilton, Virginia. *W.E.B. DuBois, a Biography.* New York: Crowell, 1972.

Hughes, Langston. *Fight for Freedom: The Story of the NAACP.* New York: Norton, 1962.

Jay, David. *Growing Up Black.* New York: Morrow, 1968.

Thornburg, Emma Lou. *Booker T. Washington.* New York: Prentice, 1969.

Watson, Denton L. *Lion in the Lobby: Clarence Mitchell Jr.'s Struggle for the Passage of Civil Rights Laws.* New York: Morrow, 1991.

Appendix A:
TEXT OF THE CALL

THE CALL

A Lincoln Emancipation Conference

February 12, 1909

To Discuss Means for Securing Political and
Civil Equality for the Negro

The celebration of the centennial of the birth of
Abraham Lincoln, widespread and grateful as it may
be, will fail to justify itself if it takes no note and
makes no recognition of the colored men and women
to whom the great emancipator labored to assure freedom. Besides a day of rejoicing, Lincoln's birthday in
1909 should be one of taking stock of the nation's
progress since 1865. How far has it lived up to the obli-
gations imposed upon it by the Emancipation Proclamation? How far has it gone in assuring each and
every citizen, irrespective of color, the equality of op-

portunity and equality before the law, which underlie our American institutions and are guaranteed by the Constitution?

If Mr. Lincoln could revisit this country, he would be disheartened by the nation's failure in this respect. He would learn that on January 1, 1909, Georgia had rounded out a new oligarchy by disfranchising the Negro after the manner of all other Southern states. He would learn that the Supreme Court of the United States, designed to be a bulwark of American liberties, had failed to meet several opportunities to pass squarely upon this disfranchisement of millions by laws avowedly discriminatory and openly enforced in such manner that white men may vote and black men be without a vote in their government; he would discover, therefore that taxation without representation is the lot of millions of wealth-producing American citizens, in whose hands rests the economic progress and welfare of an entire section of the country. He would learn that the Supreme Court, according to the official statement of one of its own judges in the Berea College case, has laid down the principle that if an individual State chooses it may "make it a crime for white and colored persons to frequent the same market place at the same time, or appear in an assemblage of citizens convened to consider questions of a public or political nature in which all citizens, without regard to race, are equally interested." In many States, Lincoln would find justice enforced, if at all, by judges elected by one element in a community to pass upon the liberties and lives of another. He would see the black men and women, for whose freedom a hundred thousand of soldiers gave their lives, set apart in trains, in which they pay first class fares for third class service, and segregated in railway stations and in places of entertainment; he would observe that State after State declines to do its elementary duty in preparing the Negro through education for the best exercise of citizenship.

Added to this, the spread of lawless attacks upon the Negro, North, South and West—even in the Springfield made famous by Lincoln—often accompanied by revolting brutalities, sparing neither sex, nor age nor youth, could not but shock the author of the sentiment that "government of the people, by the people, for the people shall not perish from the earth."

Silence under these conditions means tacit approval. The indifference of the North is already responsible for more than one assault upon democracy, and every such attack reacts as unfavorably upon whites as upon blacks. Discrimination once permitted cannot be bridled; recent history in the South shows that in forging chains for the Negroes, the white voters are forging chains for themselves. "A house divided against itself cannot stand"; this government cannot exist half-slave and half-free any better today than it could in 1861. Hence we call upon all believers in democracy to join in a national conference for the discussion of present evils, the voicing of protests, and the renewal of the struggle for civil and political liberty.

Resolutions
Adopted by the National Negro Committee
June 1, 1909

We denounce the ever-growing oppression of our 10,000,000 colored fellow citizens as the greatest menace that threatens the country. Often plundered of their just share of the public funds, robbed of nearly all part in the government, segregated by common carriers, some murdered with impunity, and all treated with open contempt by officials, they are held in some

States in practical slavery to the white community. The systematic persecution of law-abiding citizens and their disfranchisement on account of their race alone is a crime that will ultimately drag down to an infamous end any nation that allows it to be practiced, and it bears most heavily on those poor white farmers and laborers whose economic position is most similar to that of the persecuted race.

The nearest hope lies in the immediate and patiently continued enlightenment of the people who have been inveigled into a campaign of oppression. The spoils of persecution should not go to enrich any class or classes of the population. Indeed persecution of organized workers, peonage, enslavement of prisoners, and even disfranchisement already threaten large bodies of whites in many southern states.

We fully agree with the prevailing opinion that the transformation of the unskilled colored laborers in industry and agriculture into skilled workers is of vital importance to that race and to the nation, but we demand for the Negroes, as for all others, a free and complete education, whether by city, state, or nation, a grammar school and industrial training for all, and technical, professional, and academic education for the most gifted.

But the public schools assigned to the Negro of whatever kind or grade will never receive a fair and equal treatment until he is given equal treatment in the Legislature and before the law. Nor will the practically educated Negro, no matter how valuable to the community he may prove, be given a fair return for his labor or encouraged to put forth his best efforts or given the chance to develop that efficiency that comes only outside the school until he is respected in his legal rights as a man and a citizen.

We regard with grave concern the attempt manifest South and North to deny to black men the right to work and to enforce this demand by violence and bloodshed. Such a question is too fundamental and clear even to be submitted to arbitration. The late strike in Georgia is not simply a demand that Negroes be displaced, but that proven and efficient men be made to surrender their long followed means of livelihood to white competitors.

As first and immediate steps toward remedying these national wrongs, so full of peril for whites as well as the blacks of all sections, we demand of Congress and the Executive:

1. That the Constitution be strictly enforced and the civil rights guaranteed under the Fourteenth Amendment be secured impartially to all.
2. That there be equal educational opportunities for all and in all the States, and that public school expenditure be the same for the Negro and white child.
3. That in accordance with the Fifteenth Amendment the right of the Negro to the ballot on the same terms as other citizens be recognized in every part of the country.

The committee on permanent organization in its report proposed a resolution providing for "the incorporation of a national committee to be known as a Committee for the Advancement of the Negro Race, to aid their progress and make their citizenship a reality, with all the rights and privileges pertaining thereto." It presented also a resolution calling for a committee of forty charged with the organization of a national committee with the power to call the convention in 1910.

We deplore any recognition of, or concession to, prejudice or color by the federal government in any officer or branch thereof, as well as the presidential declaration on the appointment of colored men to office in the South, contradicting as it does the President's just and admirable utterance against the proposed disfranchisement of the colored voters of Maryland.

Appendix B:
NAACP EXECUTIVE SECRETARIES AND EXECUTIVE DIRECTORS

Executive Secretaries/NAACP

Frances Blascoer	1910–1911
Mary Ovington	1911–1912
May Nerney	1912–1916
Royal Nash	1916–1917
John Shillady	1918–1920
James Weldon Johnson	1920–1930

Executive Directors/NAACP

Walter White	1930–1955
Roy Wilkins	1955–1977
Benjamin Hooks	1977–1992

INDEX

ABOUT THE AUTHOR

Jacqueline L. Harris has degrees in chemistry/ bacteriology and journalism and has worked as a medical technologist, serving on the SS *Hope* hospital ship, science and medical writer, science editor, and editor with a utility company. She is the author or coauthor of seven previous books for young readers, including *Marching to Freedom: The Life of Martin Luther King, Jr., Nine Black American Doctors, Martin Luther King, Jr., Science in Ancient Rome,* and *Henry Ford.* Ms. Harris was born in Ohio and now makes her home in Connecticut.